AROUND INDIA'S FIRST TABLE

Around India's First Table

Dining & Entertaining at the Rashtrapati Bhavan

Lizzie Collingham with Salma Husain

Photography by Dheeraj Paul

Published by Publications Division, Government of India

LEFT: A pair of butlers at the entrance to the banquet hall

AROUND INDIA'S FIRST TABLE

Commissioned by the President's Secretariat, Rashtrapati Bhavan, and Indira Gandhi National Centre for the Arts (IGNCA), Ministry of Culture, Government of India

Executed by Sahapedia

Written by Lizzie Collingham with Salma Husain

Photography by Dheeraj Paul, 2014–16

Other photo credits: Rashtrapati Bhavan Photo Section; Imperial War Museum, London; Centre for South Asian Studies, Cambridge; Mountbatten Papers, University of Southampton; Private Collection of Anshul Avijit and Machindra Kasture; and Dinesh Khanna

Resource Persons: Gaitri Issar Kumar, joint secretary-cum-social secretary to the president, and Captain Prashant Singh, comptroller of the president's household

Researchers: Suchismita Chattopadhyay, Habiba Insaf and Ram Niwas Singh

Editorial Consultants: Sudha Gopalakrishnan and Yashaswini Chandra

Copy Editors: Aruna Ghose and Yashaswini Chandra

Designed by Malini Saigal

Production Coordination: V. K. Meena, Publications Division

Printed by Thomson Press India Ltd.

Price: ₹ 1185.00

PD BN ISBN: 978-81-230-2128-7
RB-ENG-OP-013-2016-17

Published by Additional Director General
Publications Division
Ministry of Information & Broadcasting
Government of India

CONTENTS

Photo credit: Dinesh Khanna

सत्यमेव जयते

PRESIDENT

REPUBLIC OF INDIA

FOREWORD

This volume celebrates the tradition of hospitality that the Rashtrapati Bhavan, as the premier home of the Indian Republic, is known for. It is 'around India's first table', that the convivial side of Indian diplomacy is on display. The Rashtrapati Bhavan is the first port of call for visiting heads of state and it is at the state banquets that our eminent guests have been welcomed and felicitated.

More guests are entertained at the Rashtrapati Bhavan at luncheons, at-homes and receptions. The annual at-home receptions celebrating India's Independence and the establishment of the republic and the reception to honour freedom fighters are special moments in the calendar of the Rashtrapati Bhavan. It has been a delight for me to host our honoured guests.

Since the colonial period when largely European cuisine was served at the Viceroy's House, the menus of the Rashtrapati Bhavan have come to showcase the richness and variety of Indian cuisine. The nature of hospitality has also changed to reflect the warmth intrinsic to the Indian home. This book traces this transition. Here the role of the efficient staff of the household and kitchens—from the comptroller and his deputies, the cooks, the butlers, to the support staff—down the ages is highlighted. It is on their mastery and dedication that dining and entertaining at the Rashtrapati Bhavan rests.

This book is part of a series designed to open up the Rashtrapati Bhavan and bring its interior charm closer to the general public.

I wish the book and the series well!

PRANAB MUKHERJEE
JULY 2016
RASHTRAPATI BHAVAN, NEW DELHI

Preface

This volume on the kitchens, dining and entertaining at the Rashtrapati Bhavan is part, the ninth in the series, of a multi-volume documentation project that seeks to capture and present various facets of life at the Rashtrapati Bhavan. Although stand-alone volumes on the Rashtrapati Bhavan have been published in the past, in-depth studies on different aspects of this living heritage were not available. A need was therefore felt for researching and documenting the various inter-related aspects of the Rashtrapati Bhavan into a seamlessly interwoven series of books for posterity. With this objective in mind, the President's Secretariat commissioned a documentation project to present a multi-volume series in collaboration with the Indira Gandhi National Centre for the Arts and Sahapedia.

It is impossible to overemphasise the historical, political, architectural and ecological significance of the Rashtrapati Bhavan. The erstwhile Viceroy's House, with its grandeur and immaculate richness, was initially intended to be the showpiece of British colonial power, but has undergone a radical transformation after Independence, and now represents the epicentre of the world's most populous and vibrant democracy. The official residence and office of the head of the state of India is also a meeting ground for world leaders, heads of states and other dignitaries. The architectural form of the Rashtrapati Bhavan blends western and eastern styles, as also tradition and modernity. The syncretic form of the Rashtrapati Bhavan is reflective of the very idea of India.

The present volume traces the history of dining and entertaining at the Rashtrapati Bhavan since 1931 when it was first occupied by the British viceroy to the present day, through five chapters interspersed with recent and archival photographs and signature recipes. It begins with a description of the state banquet, an event which is a central feature of the diplomatic duties of the President of India and the culmination of the kitchen and waiting staffs' hard work. Working backwards from the food served at the banquet, the account reveals the careful preparation which goes into virtually transforming the banquet hall into a 'fairyland' of sparkling silver and crystal. The second chapter describes the ceremonial nature of dining at the then Viceroy's House, the food culture, an expression of British power and prestige. The next chapter looks at the role of food at the Viceroy's House through increased British engagement with Indian nationalist leaders and negotiations towards Independence. The fourth chapter explores how a newly-independent India and its presidents negotiated the various ways of defining India and how this was expressed in the kitchens and dining arrangements of the Rashtrapati Bhavan. The final chapter highlights the Rashtrapati Bhavan as a window into the varied nature of Indian cuisine incorporating dishes and influences from different regions. It examines the role of the Rashtrapati Bhavan's kitchens in the development of such a 'national cuisine'. This brings us full circle to the state banquet with which the volume begins. Each chapter includes a signature recipe, typical of the repertoire of the Rashtrapati Bhavan but also simple enough for interested readers to try at home. The recipes reflect both the Anglo-Indian legacy and the increasingly regional variation within the Indian cuisine at the Rashtrapati Bhavan. Special photographs bring alive the food culture of the Rashtrapati Bhavan highlighting the hosts, guests, officials, chefs, cooks, butlers and staff.

I am confident that with this and the rest of the volumes of the series, our understanding of the Rashtrapati Bhavan, its centrality to the idea of a progressive and dynamic Indian state, will be enriched.

OMITA PAUL
SECRETARY TO THE PRESIDENT
JULY 2016
RASHTRAPATI BHAVAN, NEW DELHI

CHAPTER 1

The State Banquet

The Indian Republic's First State Banquet

On 24 January 1950 Indrani Jagjivan Ram attended her first state banquet at Government House, New Delhi. That morning the constituent assembly had signed India's new constitution. On this symbolic occasion, the 'palace', which had been built as an emblem of British power, cast its aura of splendour over the meeting of the heads of two of the first Asian countries to throw off the yoke of colonial rule. Governor General Chakravarti Rajagopalachari was the first Indian to occupy the office after the British had departed in August 1947. His guest, President Sukarno of Indonesia, had led his country's struggle for freedom. The Dutch had acknowledged Indonesia's independence just one month previously, in December 1949. The Indonesian president had come to India to celebrate India's first Republic Day.

Indrani and her husband were greeted at the guest entrance by two finely dressed ushers and directed along a corridor lined with the Governor General's Bodyguard (GGBG), standing so still that they resembled lifeless statues.[1] When they reached the Ashoka Hall they found a crowd of well-dressed guests milling about with butlers moving among them carrying trays of colourful sherbets in tiny glasses. A short while later a voice called, 'Attention!' Everyone obediently formed a neat line. The band played the Indonesian national anthem, followed by the 'Jana Gana Mana' and Governor General Rajagopalachari and President Sukarno glided into the room. They moved along the line of guests, shaking hands and exchanging a few words with each of them on their way to the dining room.

Indrani was relieved to find herself seated next to the comfortingly familiar figure of Prime Minister Jawaharlal Nehru. He reassured her that the butler would only place suitable food before her as the rose next to her plate indicated that she was vegetarian. As the band began to play and everyone began to eat their cream of spinach soup, he explained how the proceedings worked: 'See those tiny green and red bulbs on the wall in front of you—when each course commences the green light will be on and the bearers will start to serve the food. And when the course finishes, the red light will flash, signalling bearers to start clearing up the table. See now the red light is on, now the bearer will take our plates away.' Indrani listened politely but asked herself for how long were Indians going to be proud of adopting British manners now that the departure of the British meant the end of India's slavery.[2]

The President's Bodyguard march into position

LEFT: The staircase designed as the viceroy's private stairway as it was in 1931 when the Viceroy's House was just completed [Source: Centre for South Asian Studies]; FACING PAGE: The President's Bodyguard in ceremonial uniform line the route to the Ashoka Hall impressing visitors with their motionless pose

In fact, what Indrani was witnessing was not so much an act of imitation but of appropriation. Walking in the grounds of the magnificent building when it was still the Viceroy's House, Mahatma Gandhi had told the viceroy, Lord Mountbatten, that it was far too big for one man. It would have to be turned into a museum or college once the British had finally departed. Mountbatten protested that India would be the largest democracy in Asia. The eyes of the world would be upon her. Other heads of state would come and visit and India would need to entertain and impress them.[3] This was precisely the way in which the new Indian prime minister and his governor general were using the house in January 1950. The cloak of splendour which the house had thrown over the Raj was now being used to lend grandeur to the new Indian Republic. In fact, Indrani's husband, Jagjivan Ram, was the youngest minister in Nehru's interim cabinet. In those early days, just two years after Independence, the principal aim was to demonstrate that the Indian state had mastered, and could effectively deploy, the conventions which governed state occasions. India was not simply aping viceregal rituals but showing that it was fluent in the diplomatic language of state protocol in which all nations needed to be conversant. The success of the banquet affirmed that India could proudly take its rightful place on the international stage. Today, guests at a state banquet at the Rashtrapati Bhavan experience a ritual which echoes the viceregal past but which the Indian state has quietly but emphatically made its own.

Guests arriving at the Rashtrapati Bhavan for a state banquet ascend to the main floor by means of a marble staircase which was designed as the viceroy's private stairway. On either side of the staircase, troughs lined with black marble catch water which spouts from stone lions' heads set on the walls.[4] The President's Bodyguard (PBG) lining the guests' route look every bit as impressive as the motionless Sikh lancers who stood in the corridors like grim stone giants when the French socialite Baron Jean Pellenc attended a viceregal ball in 1935.[5]

The ceremony of greeting the President of India and his guests has been modified since the early days when Indrani experienced her first banquet. It is now the guests who walk up to the president after their name has been announced. The mode of entering the dining room has also been altered since the early days after Indian Independence. The guests now file in first. Once everyone is standing solemnly behind their chairs, the President of India and his guests of honour walk to their places along the space between the table and the chairs. Only once the president has taken his seat at the centre of the table does everyone else sit down. Political precedence is still carefully observed, just as it was in the days of the Raj, with the president at the apex of the triangle and the guests ranged along the table in order of their place in the political hierarchy.

Preparing a State Banquet

An ex-butler described the state dining room laid for a banquet as a 'sparkling fairyland'. The guests enter the same beautifully proportioned banquet hall, panelled in teak, softly lit by concealed lighting and four crystal chandeliers hanging from the cream-coloured arched ceiling that was admired by Sir Francis Cannon Tudsbery when he visited the viceroy, Lord Linlithgow, in 1939.[6] Important changes have made the room representative of the Indian state. The portraits that line the walls are now of former presidents rather than viceroys and the frieze above the cornice is now hung with embroideries of Indian design. The display of gold rose-bowls, cups and dishes which were presented to the king by the London Company of Goldsmiths and Silversmiths as a gesture of fealty to the empire have been replaced by a portrait of Mahatma Gandhi. But the scene is every bit as dazzling as it was for Francis Tudsbery. At every banquet, the colour scheme is carefully chosen to match the colours of the guest nation's flag. On 25 March 2015, the red table runner and the maroon napkins were to honour the emir of Qatar. Red and yellow roses decorated the table. The gold plates gleamed, the crystal caught the light from the candles placed at intervals along the table, and pink watermelon and bright orange juice glowed in the glasses. Little bowls of dahi gujya next to each plate were elegantly decorated with swirls of chilli sauce and jewel-like pomegranate seeds. Interspersed along the table were small dishes of dried fruit, chocolates and crystallised ginger ready for the dessert course at the end of the meal.

After the speeches were over, the guests settled down to savour the fruits of several days' labour in the kitchens of the Rashtrapati Bhavan. The chef and his team had planned and prepared for the banquet over several weeks. During the planning stage, each cook had been allotted responsibility for a particular dish and after a brief meeting on the morning of 25 March they set to work to prepare the banquet. The atmosphere which prevails in the Rashtrapati Bhavan kitchens is one of quiet efficiency. The longest serving cooks and bakers have been employed here for as many as 40 years and over the course of time they have learned how to work well together as a team. Once they have agreed on the plan of work for the day, the cooks use their own initiative to get on with the preparations. On 25 March, there were no other functions taking place in the Rashtrapati Bhavan so the cooks and bakers were able to concentrate fully on preparations for the banquet. Unlike a restaurant kitchen, where specialist cooks tend to be employed to carry out specific kitchen tasks such as butchery, and where most cooks are only expected to produce one particular type of dish, such as Chinese or Mughlai, cooks at the Rashtrapati Bhavan are all-rounders. They have honed their culinary skills

RIGHT: The table as it looked to guests as they entered the banquet hall on 25 March 2015 for the banquet in honour of the emir of Qatar

through years of practice. Naturally they have particular strengths but most can pitch in and cook virtually any dish while the bakers can make the entire Rashtrapati Bhavan repertoire of puddings and cakes.[7] As the young assistant cook Vikash noted, in the Rashtrapati Bhavan kitchens one day a cook might be asked to fix a salad, the next to make the dressing. An order sometimes comes down to the kitchen from the president's family quarters and then he finds himself cooking an unfamiliar Bengali fish dish. Vikash trained at the Ashoka Hotel in the Mughlai Awadhi section. Since coming to the Rashtrapati Bhavan his skills have widened and he has learned to make and dress salads, garnish continental dishes and operate a tandoor.[8]

On 25 March, Sanjay Kumar mixed bread dough and Mahesh Singh began by grinding the lentils to make the dahi gujya. He then joined Minhaj Ali, Mohan Ram and Daman Prakash who were peeling potatoes and hulling pointed gourds in order to make potol dorma. Basheer Ahmed minced mutton for kebabs. R. Rajagopal, the head cook, quietly began his patrol of the kitchens, a menu and list of tasks in hand. In an earlier preparatory meeting he and the chef had discussed the order in which each dish should be prepared according to perishability. On the appointed day it was his responsibility to ensure that the preparations went according to plan.

CLOCKWISE FROM ABOVE: *R. Rajagopal, the chief cook, on his tour of the kitchens, makes sure that the preparations for the banquet are on schedule. He trained as a cook at the navy catering school at Hamla, Mumbai. After he left the navy he worked for K.R. Narayanan when he was vice president and came to the Rashtrapati Bhavan in 1997 when he became president; Mahesh Singh fries the lentil dumplings for the dahi gujya; Minhaj Ali, Mahesh Singh, Mohan Ram and Daman Prakash prepare potol dorma. This dish of pointed gourds stuffed with potatoes and cooked in an onion-tomato gravy is a Bengali favourite. It was included on the menu to honour President Pranab Mukherjee's home region. Minhaj Ali is one of the Rashtrapati Bhavan's longest-serving cooks having worked there for 42 years. He particularly enjoys making the sauces which are the basis for cordon bleu continental cuisine; Chef Machindra Kasture, Ajay Kanojya and Sanjay Kumar prepare the bread for the banquet*

Galouti Kebabs

These melt-in-the-mouth kebabs are a speciality of the Rashtrapati Bhavan kitchens

Ingredients

500g minced mutton ♦ 100g raw papaya paste ♦ 1 tsp ginger paste ♦ 2 tsp garlic paste ♦ 1 inch stick of cinnamon ♦ 2 green cardamom pods ♦ 4 cloves ♦ 6 peppercorns ♦ ¼ tsp nutmeg powder ♦ ¼ tsp mace powder ♦ 50g brown onion paste ♦ 2 green chillies ♦ bunch of chopped coriander leaves ♦ 3 tsp roasted gram flour ♦ 1 egg white ♦ salt to taste ♦ 1 tbsp lemon juice and lemon wedge

Method

Gently cook the minced mutton.
Take the cooked minced mutton and add raw papaya paste, ginger paste, garlic paste and salt to taste.
Leave aside for one hour.
Freshly grind cinnamon, cardamom pods, cloves, and peppercorns.
Add nutmeg and mace powder to the spice masala.
Add the spice masala to the marinated mince mixture with brown onion paste, green chillies and coriander leaves, gram flour and egg white.
Mix well to make a smooth paste.
Divide into 19 equal parts and shape into patties.
Shallow fry on a hot griddle.
Squeeze over lemon juice and serve with lemon wedges and onion rings.

Prabhat Kumar mixes the mutton and spices to make the galouti kebabs

By 10 o'clock, work in the kitchens was in full swing. The main kitchen of the Rashtrapati Bhavan is divided into two halves. On one side, Mahesh, having made a batter with the ground lentils, salt and baking powder, was deep-frying the lentil dumplings in a wok. Kiran Kumar Bhardwaj was keeping an eye on a pan of black lentils boiling in preparation for making dal raisina while Mohammed Yameen and Daman hulled bottle gourds. Prabhat Kumar mixed mutton, gram flour and a selection of spices to make galouti kebabs, a spice trolley close to hand. Prabhat then began shaping the kebab mixture into little balls, flattening them and setting them aside in a pan. Mahesh, Minhaj and Mohan followed the same procedure with softened vegetables mixed with spices to make vegetarian sabz shami kebabs for the non-meat eaters at the banquet.

On the other side of the kitchen, the lamb for the main course simmered in its stock while Chef Machindra Kasture, Ajay Kanojya and Sanjay were busy preparing the bread, kneading the dough and shaping it into small balls.

The Rashtrapati Bhavan has three kitchens which open off a long corridor. Opposite the main kitchen, where most of the savoury dishes are prepared, is the bakery and confectionery kitchen where the bakers make bread, cakes and pastries. On the morning of the banquet, the bakers were busy rolling out pastry and preparing the curd and blueberry mixture for the cheesecake dessert. In the third, smaller, halwai kitchen, Kailash Chandra Yadav reduced milk over a fire and Gopal Chandra Bhardwaj pared pistachio nuts in preparation for assembling the dessert, chhenna payas.

ABOVE: Razi Haider and Rakesh Vaish at work in the bakery

FACING PAGE ABOVE: The kitchen corridor with its elegant green stone floor. The kitchen is on the left and the bakery is on the right. The halwai kitchen is further down the corridor FACING PAGE BELOW: Ram Murat is the present head of the bakery and confectionery kitchen. Soon after he came to work in the Rashtrapati Bhavan in 1976, he dropped the ice cream machine while he was fetching it down from its place on the shelf. It broke and he thought the angry head housekeeper was going to sack him. But Haider Ali, head baker at the time, saved him from the housekeeper's wrath; Gopal Chandra Bhardwaj pares the pistachio nuts to decorate the chenna payas; Kailash Chandra Yadav reduces the milk for the dessert of chenna payas

Meanwhile, upstairs, the butlers were busy laying the dining table to the strains of the naval jazz band who were practising that evening's programme of romantic Arabian songs. Throughout the morning their music accompanied the quiet bustle of the butlers. The band has eight versatile members who can each play at least two of the instruments: a lead and bass guitar, alto and soprano saxophone, violin, flute, keyboard and percussion. Some weeks before each banquet, they work out a set of music suitable for the guest of honour and, seated in the minstrel's gallery at the south end of the hall, they play during the banquet. However, because the guests cannot see them, many do not realise that they are listening to a live band.

ABOVE: The naval jazz band in their winter uniform outside the Rashtrapati Bhavan. From left to right: Dinesh Lama (violin), Kuldeep Singh (lead guitarist), U.V. Rao (alto sax), Rajeev Kala (in-charge), Bikram Ghale (drums), Khailun Guite (lead guitar), Scaria Jacob (keyboard), C.H. Samsan (bass guitar); RIGHT: Members of the naval jazz band practising

In the banquet hall, a cloth had been spread over the carpet to protect it as the butlers moved around. A white damask tablecloth was smoothed into place and finished with a red and gold runner. The crockery and cutlery for each place setting was ranged along the table. On a side table by a window, the butler Azeem Khan quietly folded napkins while looking out over the Mughal Garden in full springtime flower. One of the household staff pulled white covers over the chairs. A door at the end of the banquet hall leads into the butler's pantry from where the food is served. Here butlers were sorting out plates, silver sauceboats and serving dishes. Tea and coffee cups and finger bowls were laid out in preparation on side tables at 17 service stations ranged along the walls of the room. As the meal progressed, the butlers would be able to quickly provide the crockery and cutlery for the later courses from these side tables.

In the phool kothri, the flower-arranging room next door to the butler's pantry, heaps of red and yellow roses surrounded one of the gardeners who was seated cross-legged on the floor, creating the flower arrangements for the table. Fifteen gardeners at the Rashtrapati Bhavan are responsible for arranging the hundreds of roses, lilies, gladioli and anthurium, which arrive at the house from the Ghazipur flower market every Wednesday. Their work brightens the many offices and rooms at the Rashtrapati Bhavan. Like the cooks, new employees learn the art of flower arranging from their seniors who are faithful Rashtrapati Bhavan retainers. Mahender Singh, the most senior among the flower arrangers, has worked there for 32 years.

ABOVE: A view of one of the side tables in the banquet hall with finger bowls and cups and saucers laid out ready to give to the guests as the banquet progresses

After a quick lunch, the kitchen work continued at a steady pace. At one end of the main kitchen, Mohammed Yameen threaded fish marinated in a tikka sauce onto skewers and then, for the vegetarians, he made skewers of marinated bell peppers, pineapple and paneer. At the other end of the long table, the chef and Ajay cut the cooked lamb off the bone. Chef Kasture represented a new departure in the kitchens of the Rashtrapati Bhavan. He was the first chef at the palace to have been trained out of house. He learned his craft with the Indian Tourism Development Corporation (ITDC) and only came to work at the Rashtrapati Bhavan in 2007 when President Pratibha Patil was in office. When he moved on to another position in June 2015 he was succeeded by another graduate of the ITDC, Chef Montu Saini.

Traditionally the cooks are the sons of men who worked in the kitchens or elsewhere in the household. They began work in the kitchens as cooks' mates, washing and cleaning up after the senior cooks, and doing the *mise en place* kitchen work, preparing the vegetables for particular dishes, grinding the spices and making sure that all the ingredients were ready and to hand so that all the senior cooks had to do was cook the dish. The baker Razi Haider is the son of the head cook-cum-halwai Haider Ali who joined the Rashtrapati Bhavan in the 1960s. Razi began working in the kitchens as a baker's mate in 1988. After four years, he was promoted to the position of baker. Hard work and perseverance have made him into a master of cake decoration. Chief cook Minhaj Ali has worked in the kitchens for 42 years. His grandfather was a butler and his father a baker in the prime minister's household in the early days of the Indian Republic when the Rashtrapati Bhavan and prime ministerial residence shared staff.[9] Working at the Rashtrapati Bhavan has offered these men job security and they and their families benefit from living on the President's Estate with a school, a health centre and shops. This has fostered a steadfast loyalty among the older cooks and bakers who slowly worked their way up the kitchen hierarchy, learning their trade on the job. In the last 10 years, efforts have been made to leaven this homely atmosphere with professional training. The cooks are periodically sent for training at various hotels where they receive tuition in how to make dishes unfamiliar to traditional Indian cooks, such as soups and salads.

The cooks in turn teach their young assistants. When Ashish Kumar arrived to work in the Rashtrapati Bhavan kitchens in 2014, he had never even made a cup of tea. He was put to work in the scullery washing-up. The cooks taught him new skills and now he does the *mise en place* work of chopping vegetables and preparing ingredients; they have also taught him how to cook a few dishes. Ashish has taken his newfound skills home and his friends were impressed when he made chicken masala and shahi paneer for them on New Year's Eve.[10]

Chef Kasture's interest in food stemmed from when he was a small boy in Maharashtra. He would make trips to the local market with his mother. 'She taught me the sensory nature of food,' he explained. 'How to value the fresh green of leafy vegetables and to look out for tinges of yellow that indicate that they are past their best.' Whenever he begged her to buy food from a stall, she would invariably suggest that they cook the dish at home. This is how he learned to cook poha, the dish of rice flakes, sautéed onion, mustard seeds, turmeric and green chilli, which was one of his breakfast favourites. He loved the yellow colouring imparted to it by the turmeric. His mother was a master of *jugaad* or improvisation. When showing her son how to fry jalebis she did not have a cloth to spare from which to squeeze the dough into the hot oil. Instead, she showed him how to break the eye out of a coconut shell and use that. When it was time to choose a career, Kasture surveyed his older brothers' choices—engineer, policeman—and chose chef.[11]

The chefs at the Rashtrapati Bhavan are always eager to try out new techniques and flavour combinations. New dishes are tasted at regular intervals by a panel of those responsible for the food at the Rashtrapati Bhavan. The secretary to the president, Omita Paul, heads the panel, which includes the comptroller of the president's household, Captain Prashant Singh, and the additional comptroller of the president's household, Anita Bimal. The comptroller is responsible for the smooth running of the household and sanitation departments, from day-to-day problems to the efficient staging of the many events which take place at the palace such as swearing-in ceremonies, at-homes and governors' conferences. As

ABOVE: Dharmendra, a gardener sets out the flower arrangements at a banquet in honour of President Françoise Hollande. The arrangements were of red and white gladioli, white lilies, red carnations and blue orchids in reference to the French flag

LEFT: Chef Kasture and trainee Ajay Kanojya prepare the leg of lamb

Anjeer ka Kofta (Fig Kofta Curry)

Visitors and staff all mention this fig kofta curry as one of their favourite Rashtrapati Bhavan dishes

Ingredients

For the potato koftas

2 large potatoes ♦ ¼ tsp cornflour ♦ 100g cottage cheese ♦ salt and pepper to taste

For the fig stuffing

5 dried figs soaked in warm water for 30 minutes ♦ pinch of chaat masala ♦ ½ tsp cumin powder ♦ ½ tsp grated fresh ginger ♦ chopped green chillies to taste ♦ 1 tsp lemon juice ♦ bunch of chopped coriander leaves ♦ oil for frying

For the gravy

1 onion, finely chopped ♦ 2 tsp ginger and garlic paste ♦ chopped green chillies to taste ♦ ¼ tsp red chilli powder ♦ ½ tsp cumin powder ♦ 1 tsp coriander powder ♦ ¼ tsp turmeric ♦ ¼ tsp garam masala ♦ ground black pepper to taste ♦ 1 cup yoghurt ♦ 25 ground cashew nuts ♦ salt to taste ♦ bunch of chopped coriander leaves

Method

To make the koftas

Boil potatoes and allow to cool.
Grate the boiled potatoes and mix with cornflour and cottage cheese.
Divide the mixture into 8–10 pieces and shape into balls.
Finely chop the soaked figs and mix with a pinch of chat masala, cumin powder, grated fresh ginger, chopped green chillies, lemon juice and coriander leaves and shape into 8–10 small balls.
Take a potato mixture ball and flatten it. Then put a fig ball in the centre and wrap the potato mixture around it. Deep fry the balls.

To make the gravy

Heat cooking oil in a pan and fry the onion till golden brown.
Add ginger and garlic paste, green chillies, red chilli powder, cumin powder, coriander powder, turmeric, garam masala and pepper, and fry gently.
Whisk the yoghurt and add to the mixture a little at a time, stirring continuously to avoid curdling.
Add salt and the ground cashew nuts.
Stir and simmer on a low heat for 10–15 minutes until the masala comes away from the side of the pan.
Add a little water and simmer for 5–7 minutes.
Stir through the coriander leaves.
Arrange the fried potato-fig balls on a serving dish and pour the gravy over them.

ABOVE LEFT: *A line of photographs of his predecessors look down at Captain Prashant Singh from the wall in the office of the comptroller of the household;* TOP RIGHT: *Anita Bimal, the additional comptroller, with butlers in the banquet hall;* ABOVE: *The catering department. The comptroller, Captain Prashant Singh, and the additional comptroller, Anita Bimal stand in the middle. They are flanked on the left by the executive chef, Montu Saini, and on the right by the section officer in charge of the household, V.K. Narang, and the naval catering supervisor, Murli Nair. The cooks and bakers stand behind*

CLOCKWISE FROM LEFT: Preparing a thali; Sanjay Kumar, a senior cook and Daman, a MTS cook mate prepare the food for the tasting session under the watchful eye of the chief cook, R. Rajagopal; Omita Paul, the secretary to the president, Captain Prashant Singh, the comptroller, and Anita Bimal, the additional comptroller, with Chef Montu Saini at a tasting session; The Club des Chefs des Chefs meet American President Barack Obama at the White House. Chef Kasture is the fourth from the left in the front row [Source: Machindra Kasture]

the household section includes the kitchens, it is the comptroller who ensures that the food for every occasion is of the highest quality. It might be expected that Captain Singh's previous experience as the commanding officer of INS *Gomantak* in Goa equipped him with the necessary skills to be an effective comptroller. However, at the Rashtrapati Bhavan, he found a very different environment from the one he was used to. It was his experience in managing people that stood him in good stead. The job requires the ability to make the most of available resources, an eye for detail and an imperturbable good humour.[12]

The food-tasting panel gathers together around a table of sample dishes and carefully tries each one. They discuss its merits in terms of colour, taste and presentation. Some dishes are sent back to the chef with suggestions for refinement, others are approved and added to the Rashtrapati Bhavan repertoire of dishes.

A great deal of thought goes into the planning of the menu for state banquets. The ministry of external affairs sends the President's Secretariat notice of proposed visits, the likes and dislikes, and any food allergies of the visiting dignitary, as well as a suggested guest list. Captain Singh and the chef put the menu together, with suggestions from the secretary to the president. Other officers sometimes get involved and, at present, the social secretary to the president, Gaitri Issar Kumar, a connoisseur of food, also guides the kitchens in deciding on the menu for state events. The dishes chosen

reflect the tastes of the visiting dignitary's country. The menu for the emir of Qatar on 25 March 2015 was heavy on mutton reflecting the Arabian liking for meat. At an earlier banquet for the vegetarian president of Sri Lanka, the menu was mostly vegetarian. Gaitri Kumar explained that if a South Asian dignitary is visiting then the kitchen goes 'all out' with a range of spicy dishes while, with Europeans, they try not to overwhelm them with too many unfamiliar bowls of spicy gravy. When planning the meal, the comptroller and the chef pay close attention to the range of ingredients, colours and textures across the various dishes. Great care is taken to present light food, rather than the thick and oily curries which can give Indian cuisine a bad name, although the food does tend to be richer than normal fare. For this reason they are careful to choose a light soup to start the meal. A Rashtrapati Bhavan favourite is the delicate almond soup, seasoned with curry leaves, garlic and green chilli, which was served to the emir of Qatar.

The executive chef at the Rashtrapati Bhavan is a member of the Club des Chefs des Chefs, a society whose members are the chefs for various heads of state. Its members meet in a different country each year where they have the chance to experience executive cuisine in other countries. This is a rare opportunity as chefs are normally left at home when their president or prime minister travels. As a member of the club, Chef Kasture had the opportunity to discuss culinary matters with his peers and compare the kitchens of the Rashtrapati Bhavan with the kitchens of Buckingham Palace and the White House. One aspect of the White House tradition which particularly appealed to him was the use of edible flowers as a garnish.

The chef's concern with presentation was evident at the banquet for the emir of Qatar. Once all the meat had been sliced off the roast leg of lamb the meat was arranged around the bones which were carefully decorated with silver foil. The chef then prepared a sauce espagnole using the strained stock in which the lamb had been simmering that morning. Sauce espagnole was one of Auguste Escoffier's five mother sauces which he used as the foundation for almost all savoury dishes. A celebrated chef who worked for César Ritz and at the Savoy Hotel in London in the 1890s, Escoffier wrote the treatise *La Guide Culinaire* (1903) which has ever since served as one of the authoritative

texts for those learning classic French cookery. The chef's competence in preparing the sauce betrayed his training as a chef, grounded in the basics of French, as well as Indian cookery.

Chef Saini has had the same training in the essential skills associated with European and Indian cuisine. As soon as he joined the ITDC training programme he opted to train as a chef and put in three years of hard work perfecting his skills in the kitchen, bakery and confectionery departments. He qualified as a chef in 2007 and since then has worked in commercial kitchens while acquiring a string of post-graduate qualifications. At only 34 he brings youthful exuberance to his new position and is full of plans for the future. He convinced the appointments panel that he was the right chef for the job when in the June heat of 2015 he prepared for them a refreshing cold beetroot and melon soup. He has introduced new dishes to the Rashtrapati Bhavan, among them his own signature lamb dish, darbari gosht, consisting of a blend of a fine lamb stock with lamb slow-cooked in the dum style and a masala of spices with a strong note of fennel.[13]

On the afternoon of 25 March 2015, while the chef dribbled his tasty espagnole sauce over the leg of lamb, Basheer cooked the galouti and sabz shami kebabs over a hot griddle in the corner and fetched the lauki nazarat (stuffed bottle gourds) out of the oven, while Mohammed cooked the moti-e-zamin and fish tikka skewers in the tandoor. In the adjoining half of the kitchen, the little glass bowls of dahi gujya were prepared, while across the corridor in the bakery, Gaurav Kaushal put the final touches to the blueberry cheesecake dessert. Meanwhile, in the halwai kitchen, Kailash carefully took the cheese curd dumplings, which he and Gopal had made that morning from the sugar syrup in which they had been simmering and placed them in bowls of thickened milk flavoured with cardamom.

CLOCKWISE FROM LEFT: Basheer Ahmed takes the roundels of stuffed bottle gourd out of the oven. They are now ready to be simmered in a tomato gravy; Preparing the dahi gujya: a lentil dumpling was placed in each bowl and then yoghurt was poured on top. Each bowl was decorated with a scattering of pomegranate seeds and a drizzle of chilli oil; Chef Kasture dribbles sauce espagnole over the lamb; The new chef at the Rashtrapati Bhavan, Montu Saini

LEFT: Butlers lay the table for the banquet in honour of the emir of Qatar. The band could be heard practising while the butlers set the table in an atmosphere of calm concentration; ABOVE LEFT: Anita Bimal, additional comptroller, tastes the food before the banquet; ABOVE RIGHT: *Household staff pour the drinks just before the banquet*

Upstairs in the banquet hall, the laying of the table continued. By now the butlers had carefully arranged each place setting at an equal distance from the edge of the table and each other. Using strings, they were careful to ensure that all the place settings were in line. The arrangement of plate, knives and forks and glasses was absolutely precise. The flower arrangements were ranged along the length of the table interspersed with candles in glass sconces. Two men placed the chairs exactly with the help of another string.

Downstairs in the kitchens, pots and pans of all the dishes were lined up in preparation for the final tasting. At a quarter to six, Bimal arrived in the kitchens. Presented with a small bowl of each of the different dishes, she tried a teaspoon of each and either approved them or suggested an adjustment to the seasoning. This ritual of the final tasting is performed before every banquet, either by the additional comptroller, or the comptroller himself, to ensure that the food leaves the kitchen at its best. Once the tasting was over and a few final touches had been added, the kitchen bustled with cooks covering the food and loading it onto trolleys to take up to the butler's pantry from where it would be served.

The butler's pantry and the banquet hall now became the focus of activity. The section officer in charge of the household, V.K. Narang, and the naval catering supervisor, Murli Nair, appeared and began to count the plates and supervise the preparation of the food as it was ladled into serving dishes, covered in foil and placed in the warming ovens. The chef darted about the pantry checking if everything was in order. In the banquet hall, aides-de-camp (ADCs) began to appear, checking the seating plan so that they could be sure to efficiently guide the guests to their chairs. As the PBG started to take their places on the guests' route into the Ashoka Hall, the butlers bustled in and out of the pantry with jugs of watermelon and orange juice, filling the glasses at each place setting. The band leader came down from the gallery to check sound levels while technicians checked the president and the emir's microphones set out at their places ready for the speeches. Behind a wooden screen, sound and light engineers checked that all the lights were working, that sound levels were just right and that the temperature of the room was comfortable. ADCs for the president and his guest of honour gathered around their seats to confirm that everything was in order. It is an ADC's job to brief the president about all the minor technicalities of every situation and remind him of the correct protocol. At the banquets they ensure that his microphone is working, and that his speech and a glass of water are to hand. The job of the ADCs is to free the president from trivial organisational concerns so that he can concentrate on the more important task of diplomacy.

By quarter to eight, the guests were being presented to the president in the Ashoka Hall, the catering officers, Nair and Sunil N.S., and cooks were beginning to remove the food from the hot ovens. For the chef, this is the most stressful part of the preparations for a banquet. He darted around the butler's pantry making sure that the bread would arrive

LEFT: Freedom fighters at the annual at-home in their honour on 9 August 2015; ABOVE: Razi Haider exemplifies the family atmosphere which prevails in the Rashtrapati Bhavan. Even while the kitchens were bustling with preparations for the banquet, he was busy baking various birthday cakes for people on the president's staff. He explained that because his father was such a proficient cook and halwai he sought out a skill at which he alone could excel and began his career of baking and decorating magnificent cakes

hot at the table, that last-minute garnishes were added and that the presentation of every dish was just right. Despite the last-minute anxiety, the atmosphere of calm in the Rashtrapati Bhavan kitchens is striking. The kitchens are quite different from noisy, over-heated, bad-tempered hotel or restaurant kitchens. Although the chef was firm with his staff, he was also aware that the cooks, many of them having been trained in the Rashtrapati Bhavan, would be alienated by the bad temper of a celebrity-style chef. A friendly atmosphere of camaraderie prevails in the kitchens. There is little haughtiness on the part of the senior staff towards their juniors.[14] They are eager to pass on their culinary skills and Rashtrapati Bhavan traditions, to the next generation. The Rashtrapati Bhavan is not just a state building, it is also the home of the President of India. This is something of which all the staff are very conscious. They are keen to demonstrate that they can produce a fine feast, not in the distant, grand manner of a hotel, but as a display of hospitality at the most prestigious home in India.

At precisely a quarter past eight, the 82 guests began to file into the banquet hall. Once the speeches by the president and the emir were over, the butlers hurried in bearing bowls of almond soup. From the guests' perspective the service at the banquets is superb. The butlers at the Rashtrapati Bhavan are masters of their art, attentive to the guests without being intrusive. Observed from above, dressed in their smart black suits with red piping, they appear to be engaged in a military operation. As Prime Minister Nehru explained to Indrani Jagjivan Ram in 1950, the butlers are coordinated by three lights above each portrait around the walls of the room. The blue light indicates that they should stand by, the green that they should start serving. The various dishes are offered to the diners using the 'butler service' method. They offer the serving platters to the guests who help themselves to the food. Each butler is allocated about six guests to look after, with a personal butler waiting on the president and his guest of honour. When the head butler switches on the red light, all the butlers take a step forward and begin clearing away the plates.

The band is also governed by the lights and when the red light begins to flash in the minstrel's gallery the bandleader signals for the music to fade out. For regulars at the Rashtrapati Bhavan the music is a useful cue. The head butler sets the pace of the meal according to the president. This tradition of organising the meal in accordance with the pace of the president is inherited from the viceroys who themselves adopted it from the English monarchy. Today the pages waiting on the royal table at Buckingham Palace are coordinated by blue and amber lights and the pace of the meal is set by the monarch. During Queen Victoria's reign, state dinners were hasty affairs as Victoria was notorious for gobbling her food and everyone was expected to stop eating as soon as the queen did.[15] At the Rashtrapati Bhavan, naval ADC Lieutenant Commander Rakesh Yadav has witnessed some bewildered guests caught out by this convention. Unfamiliar with Rashtrapati Bhavan customs, deep in conversation with their neighbour for the last 15 minutes, as the music fades

The naval ADC to President Pranab Mukherjee, Lieutenant Commander Rakesh Yadav, checks the microphone for the President's speech

they watch with dismay as their plate is whisked away before they have had a chance to sample even a mouthful.[16] Despite such mishaps, if the guests at a banquet become engrossed in conversation, then the banquet can be counted as a success.

Many diplomats would prefer to engage in less formal entertaining. They argue that the state banquet is an inefficient venue for conducting political business.[17] But these diplomats have missed the point. As Meira Kumar, former speaker of the Lok Sabha and author of a book on Indian parliamentary diplomacy asserts, the state banquet should be a positive part of diplomacy.[18] During the banquet, the serious matters under discussion behind closed doors can be left behind and the protagonists can talk about light-hearted subjects. Brought together over a sumptuous feast, people from different cultures can learn to accept each other and, ideally, form a bond. This makes the state banquet the supreme expression of gastronomic diplomacy. As Ernest Satow, the influential English diplomat, pointed out in his *Guide to Diplomatic Practice* (1917), state protocol such as banquets are 'a means to an end, not the end in itself'.[19] Experienced politicians understand this principle. Hillary Clinton is said to have described food as the oldest diplomatic tool while the French president, Françoise Hollande, is quoted as having told the Club des Chefs des Chefs that diplomacy is a lot more difficult, 'if you make a mess of the meal'.[20] Hollande reinstated the cheese course with which the more expedient Nicolas Sarkozy had done away. Angela Merkel, the German chancellor, also loves cheese and she and Hollande have formed a bond over their joint enjoyment of this course.[21]

Guests listen attentively to President Mukherjee's speech at the banquet in honour of the emir of Qatar

In December 1988, a thaw began in the cold relations between India and China when Li Peng, the premier of the People's Republic of China, accepted Prime Minister Rajiv Gandhi's invitation to visit India. He stayed at the Rashtrapati Bhavan and in cordial talks with R. Venkataraman discussed bilateral cooperation in trade, industry, science and technology while carefully avoiding all mention of the border issue. The highlight of the visit was a luncheon for the Chinese delegation under a shamiana in the Mughal Garden. Besides Indian dishes, the cooks had carefully prepared Chinese dishes as a compliment to their guest. Li Peng returned the compliment by taking a second helping and stating that they were the best he had eaten outside China. He visibly relaxed and chatted amiably with everyone, while his wife, Zhu Lin, plied the president with questions about the economic state of the nation. At the end of the meal she wrote on her menu card a message in Chinese wishing the president good health and success. 'Watching the bonhomie at the lunch,' observed President Venkataraman, 'one would never have suspected that there had been an interlude of bitter discord between our two countries.'[22] This was Rashtrapati Bhavan food diplomacy in action. On 25 March 2015, as the dessert was placed on the table and the guests at the banquet tucked into their blueberry cheesecakes and chenna payas, the dishevelled cooks, their aprons covered with splashes of food, were at last able to relax and head home having successfully created the conditions for the fostering of good relations between India and Qatar.

Notes

1. Indrani Jagjivan Ram, *Milestones. A Memoir* (Penguin, New Delhi, 2010), 144.
2. Ibid., 145.
3. Pamela Hicks, *India Remembered* (Pavilion, London, 2007), 122.
4. Robert Byron, 'New Delhi II—The interior of the viceroy's house', *Country Life* LXIX, No. 1795 (13 June 1931), 754-61, 758.
5. Jean Pellenc, *Diamonds and Dust. India through French Eyes* (John Murray, London, 1936), 113.
6. Diary of Sir Francis Cannon Tudsbery, Mss. Eur. F979, India Office Collections (IOC), British Library (BL), 97.
7. Interview in Hindi with Razi Haider, 4 January 2016.
8. Interview in Hindi and English with Vikash, 4 January 2016.
9. Interview in Hindi with Minhaj Ali, 4 January 2016.
10. Interview in Hindi with Ashish Kumar, 4 January 2016.
11. Interview in English with Machindra Kasture, 10 March 2015.
12. Interview in English with Captain Prashant Singh, 5 January 2016.
13. Interview in English with Montu Saini, 4 January 2016.
14. Interview with Ashish Kumar.
15. Kathryn Jones, *For the Royal Table. Dining at the Palace* (Royal Collection Publications, London, 2008),14; Charles C. Ludington, 'Drinking for approval: wine and the British court from George III to Victoria and Albert', in *Royal Taste. Food, Power and Status at the European Courts After 1789*, ed. Daniëlle de Vooght (Ashgate, Farnham, Surrey, 2011), 57–86.
16. Interview in English with Lieutenant Commander Rakesh Yadav, 17 March 2015.
17. Linda Morgan, 'Diplomatic gastronomy: style and power at the table', *Food and Foodways* 20, 2 (2012), 146–66, 150.
18. Meira Kumar, *Indian Parliamentary Diplomacy. Speaker's Perspective* (Lok Sabha Secretariat, New Delhi, 2015).
19. Ernest Satow, *Guide to Diplomatic Practice,* 1st published 1917 (Cambridge University Press, Cambridge, 2011). His guide is still used by diplomats throughout the world.
20. Elaine Sciolino, 'Club des Chefs des Chefs', *Lumière* (27 July 2013).
21. Ibid.
22. R.Venkataraman, *My Presidential Years* (Indus, New Delhi, 1994), 596–97.x

Butlers with trays of snacks prepare to serve the guests at an Independence Day at-home

CHAPTER 2

Dining with the Viceroy

The city of New Delhi was built as a monument to eternal imperial governance with the Viceroy's House at its centre as the ultimate expression of British imperial power and authority.[1] The Durbar Hall under the imposing central dome was the main stage for the glittering ceremony that characterised British rule in India. The viceroy's elegant office in the garden wing was the bureaucratic heart of the Indian government. The imperial elite was entertained in the elegant banquet hall. Edwin Lutyens' triumph was that within this imposing statement of imperialism he also succeeded in creating a luxurious and comfortable gentleman's home.[2] Behind the magnificent edifice the Viceroy's House was both a princely palace and an English country house.[3]

As a home the building had its drawbacks. Pamela Mountbatten commented that while it was 'presumably quite impressive just to come and see and go away again [it was] a compete headache to live in'.[4] The internal plan of the house was confusing and to bewildered visitors it often appeared to consist of nothing but vast corridors leading nowhere.[5] If he had not had the luck to meet the military secretary, Major Maxwell, in one of the passages, Sir Francis Cannon Tudsbery, a visitor in 1939, thought that he 'might have spent the night wandering about looking for our rooms!'[6] However, the viceroys who lived there tended to grow fond of the building. Lutyens had paid great attention to the living quarters, and created panelled drawing rooms and small dining rooms with cosy fireplaces and views over the Mughal Garden, full of English flowers, which made it reminiscent of an English country garden. When he arrived at the Viceroy's House, ADC to Lord Mountbatten, Narendra Singh Sarila, was struck by the contrast between the 'daunting and imperious exterior' of the house and the 'cosiness of the drawing room into which I was shortly ushered. The French windows on the level of the garden terrace, with lawns and foliage beyond, made one feel as if one were in a country house rather than an immense palace'.[7] Lord Irwin grew to love the house more the longer he lived there.[8] Lord Willingdon thought it had a delightful character, while even the taciturn Lord Wavell, looking down on the house from his aeroplane, commented fondly, 'Be it never so humble, there's no place like home.'

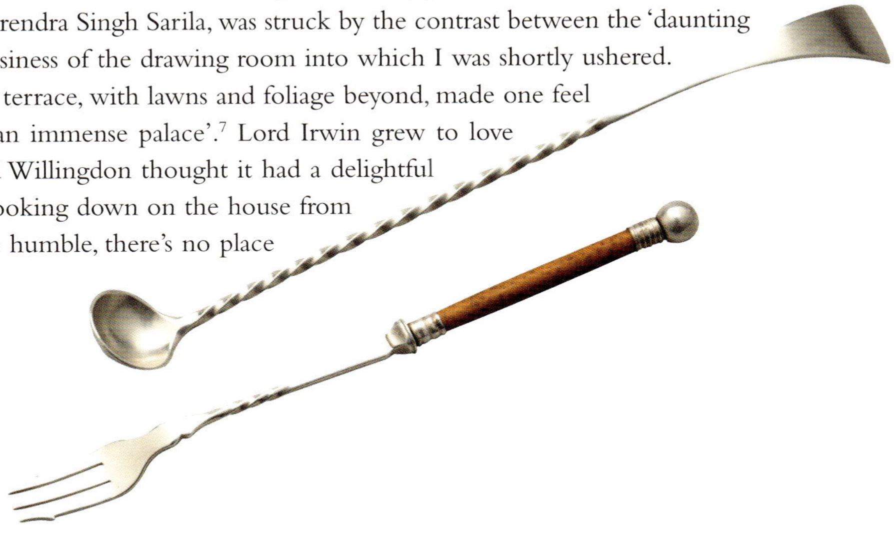

LEFT: One of the long corridors which run through the house. The viceroy's visitors searching for their bedrooms felt as though they were caught in a confusing maze

The Kitchens at the Viceroy's House

The Viceroy's House was run along the lines of Buckingham Palace, the empire's other palace-cum-home. The viceregal equivalent to Buckingham Palace's master of the household was the comptroller of the household. His department oversaw the cooking and serving of food, the wine cellar, silverware, the up-keep and cleaning of the rooms and furniture, store keeping, tailoring and laundering.[10] The comptroller, his assistant, the steward and housekeeper marshalled a battalion of about 500 cooks, bakers, confectioners, khansamas, khidmatgars, tindals, chobdars, chaprassies, masalchies, sweepers, bhistis, dhobies and syces, who looked after the viceroy and his family, the administrative staff, and an ever-changing house party of both formal state and informal personal guests. Following the pattern of a grand Palladian house, Lutyens placed the service rooms in the basement. Below the main house was a warren of kitchens, a bakery, a confectioner's kitchen, sculleries, larders, a dairy, the wine cellars, coal cellars, store rooms, linen rooms, glass and china rooms, a room devoted entirely to the maintenance of camp equipment, a tailor's shop and the viceroy's press which published the seating plans and leaflets for viceregal appointments.[11]

Surprisingly, given that among the British aristocracy a French chef was a badge of status, the kitchens at the Viceroy's House were not presided over by a European chef. In the handover document which Lord Reading prepared for Lord Irwin, the incoming viceroy, he warned 'that every attempt should be made to limit the number of European servants in India'. While Reading's butler, housekeeper, two maids, his sergeant in charge of the stables, chauffeur and gardener were all European, he eschewed a European chef. The problem, he explained with a vehemence which suggested bitter personal experience, was that European servants, when they themselves were waited upon by deferential Indian servants, tended to develop an inflated sense of their own importance. This, he advised, caused no end of trouble. In the case of a chef it meant that 'after a short time they do little or nothing and rely entirely on the staff of Cooks in the kitchen'. What was more, because they deemed themselves experts in their field they resented interference, while their ignorance of Indian ways and inability to speak Indian languages meant that, in fact, the cooks took advantage of them and withdrew far greater supplies from the stores than were really necessary. It was more efficient and less expensive, Lord Reading concluded, to place the cooks under the direct supervision of the assistant comptroller.[12] Lord Irwin appears to have heeded his advice. Indeed, no European chef was ever employed at the Viceroy's House. The presidents of India continued the tradition. It was not until Machindra Kasture was appointed in 2007 that an executive chef was put in charge of the kitchens.

A milk churn from the viceregal dairy. A dairy herd was kept on the viceregal estate, a tradition maintained by the presidents

The British were particularly keen on picnics. On display in the Kitchen Museum is the viceregal picnic box. It contained handy compartments for thermos flasks and tiffin boxes as well as straps to keep the plastic crockery and cutlery in place

The Viceroy's House must have had one of the most up-to-date kitchens in the Edwardian empire. While Lord Hardinge was still based at Government House in Calcutta, Rs 26,270 had been spent on pasteurising cans, bed and table linen, glass, kitchen utensils and crockery due to the fact that these items had been 'allowed during the Earl of Minto's Viceroyalty [1905–10] to fall very considerably below the standard required for ... Viceregal residences'.[13] When Hardinge moved into the temporary Viceregal Lodge in north Delhi in 1911 he brought the new equipment with him from Calcutta. Although it must have been an enormous undertaking to pack up the viceroy's household possessions and transport them the 1,500 kilometres from Calcutta to New Delhi, it was not an unprecedented occurrence. Every year the government of India transferred to its summer capital in Simla, and along with all the government files, the viceroy took crates of linen, crockery, kitchen utensils and the like because the viceregal lodge there was not fully equipped with a duplicate of all the viceregal household necessaries. This practice continued even after the viceroy had moved to Delhi. In his hand-over notes to Lord Irwin, Lord Reading mentioned that while each of the viceroy's houses was now equipped with its own crockery it was still necessary to take silver, cutlery and both household and table linen when moving from one to another.[14] When the viceroy moved permanently into the new palace in 1930 the kitchen equipment was transferred to the new palace. But no expense was spared in furnishing the Viceroy's House with additional equipment. Rs 8,000 of the £10,000 allocated by the new capital committee for the cost of incidental furnishings was spent on additional kitchen utensils and linen.[15] Ranged neatly on dresser shelves and stored carefully in the dresser cupboards and drawers of the new kitchens was a battery of modern culinary equipment: chafing dishes, bain-marie saucepans, mortars and pestles, mincers, seasoning boxes, graters, ladles, cleavers, knives, colanders, potato ricers, slices, spoons, tongs and scoops. The

ABOVE: The viceregal picnic basket; RIGHT: Pots and pans from the colonial period in the Kitchen Museum

ABOVE: Re-tinning the Rashtrapati Bhavan cooking pans. Mohammed Nasir rubs the heated pan with a cloth dipped in acid. He will apply the stick of tin lying on the table to the inside of the pan; LEFT: The newly-tinned pans

kitchens gleamed with shiny copper stockpots, stew pans, saucepans and sauté pans, preserving pans, braising pans, fish fryers and kettles. All were hung alongside their lids from rods conveniently placed above the kitchen ranges.[16]

Judging from a telegram sent from the viceroy's military secretary to Sir Arthur McWatters, finance secretary to the government of India, discussing the cost of the electricity used for cooking in the Viceroy's House, the ranges appear to have been state-of-the-art electric ones rather than the old-fashioned steam-run ranges the cooks would have used in Government House, Calcutta.[17] In the spacious main kitchen, the head cook and seven assistant cooks worked at chopping boards arranged along the central table with seasoning boxes, knives and assorted kitchen cutlery set out on the table top close to hand. In the bakery, well away from the heat of the stoves, the head baker and his two assistant bakers worked at marble slabs surrounded by the baking trays and patty pans, bun and cake tins, jelly, bombe and cake moulds, pastry-cutting jiggers, rolling pins, fancifully-shaped biscuit cutters, jelly bags, spatulas, egg whisks and mixing bowls, which were the tools of their trade.

The 13 cooks, bakers and confectioners were assisted by 10 kitchen assistants, a chicken cleaner, five storemen, who fetched and carried the stores for the cooks, and three water carriers. Seventeen masalchies washed and cleaned up in the sculleries. In addition, two tinmen were on the pay roll. Copper had been a favoured material for British cooking pots since the 18th century as it was an excellent conductor of heat. However, the verdigris that accumulated on copper imparted an unpleasant flavour to the food besides being extremely poisonous. It was therefore imperative that all copper kitchen utensils were coated with tin and it was the job of these tinmen to regularly apply a new protective layer.

The Rashtrapati Bhavan still uses copper cooking pots which need regular re-tinning. Mohammed Nasir visits the Bhavan once a month to perform the process using the same technique that would have been used during the days of the Raj. The pan is heated over a naked flame and then rubbed with a cloth dipped in acid. After this it is held over the fire until all residue in the pan has burned away. Then he rubs a stick of tin around the inside of the pan until it is coated in a fresh layer which is set by dipping the pan, accompanied by a satisfying hiss and plume of steam, into a sink of cold water.

The British obsession with hygiene in India meant that stringent measures were put in place in the viceroy's kitchens. Patrick Southby, ADC to Lord Linlithgow and temporary comptroller of the household, described how a policeman always sat outside the entrance to the kitchens to check that everyone entering complied with the rules. Before entering all cooks were compelled to remove their shoes and then walk through a trough of water mixed with potassium permanganate. Two bowls of disinfectant were balanced on pedestals outside the door in which they were expected to scrub their arms up to the elbow. Only once they had performed these ablutions were they allowed to enter through the door which was protected against flies by a meat-safe-style grill.[18]

The Cost of Running the Viceroy's Kitchens

Every day the kitchens produced early morning tea, breakfast, lunch, afternoon tea and dinner for the viceroy's family, the European household and administrative staff who worked in the palace, and all the houseguests. Southby commented that it was quite normal for as many as 35 people to gather round the table in the steward's room where the European staff were served their meals. Only the comptroller's assistant, who was married, was allowed to go to his quarters to eat lunch with his wife. According to Southby, when Lutyens stayed at the Viceroy's House at Lady Linlithgow's invitation (to rectify the changes Lady Willingdon had made to the decoration), he preferred to dine with the ADCs and the rest of the staff. Ironically, given the vast stage set for viceregal pomp that he had designed, he favoured the more informal atmosphere among the staff than the stiff protocol which governed all meals taken with the viceroy.

Nowadays the only members of household staff who are fed by the Rashtrapati Bhavan kitchens are the president's ADCs. Everyone else returns home to their quarters on the estate to eat their meals. For the ADCs the demands of running their own households would be an unwelcome distraction. Their job is to focus entirely on the needs of the president and so their meals are provided for them. Every three months they sit with the chef to draw up a 21-day rolling menu which the comptroller then approves. The kitchens try to make the meals varied as well as balanced. One evening the ADCs might be treated to a tandoori-themed dinner, another they might have a Chinese meal of Manchurian chicken and sweet and sour vegetables. Continental food no longer dominates the menus but on occasion they are served European-style celery soup and chicken with mushroom sauce. Lieutenant Commander Rakesh Yadav is particularly fond of the regular Monday night dinner of rajma and paneer bhurji while Major Rajesh Kumar looks forward to the Sunday evening biryani. All the ADCs feel that they need to be vigilant about their calorie consumption

ABOVE: Lieutenant Commander Rakesh Yadav, Major Rajesh Kumar, Major R.K. Banu Chander and Squadron Leader Yash Aryan, four of President Mukherjee's five ADCs, enjoying lunch in their dining room. Their favourite meal of the day is breakfast when they are served with dishes such as aloo puri, chhole bhature, parathas, eggs cooked in the style of their choosing along with toast, or south Indian uthappams and dosas

LEFT: The less formal room where the ADCs and European staff used to eat lunch [Source: Centre for South Asian Studies]

because the bakers and halwais make such good desserts. The halwais make delicious gulab jamuns which Rajesh Kumar enjoys with ice cream while Squadron Leader Yash Aryan's favourite is sabudaana kheer. An endless stream of old-fashioned cakes and puddings emerge from the bakery, the recipes for which must surely have been inherited from the viceroy's bakers and confectioners. Major R.K. Banu Chander particularly likes the trifle that is still known in the Rashtrapati Bhavan by its 1940s' name, tipsy pudding. Another of his favourites is baked alaska, while Rakesh Yadav loves the Swiss carpet roll, another Raj staple.[19]

During the cold weather there was generally an ever-changing group of the friends and family of the viceroy and his staff staying at the house. All of them had to be provided with all their meals. The constant entertaining required military-style organisation. Sir Francis Tudsbery remarked that the house bureaucracy made him feel as though he were back in his office at home. Each day a programme was placed in the guests' rooms, detailing the viceroy and vicereine's official appointments as well as the order of the social events going on in the house that day, along with a list of the invitees. The information was supplemented by printed instructions on suitable dress, timings of particular functions and the choreography of each event.[20] After breakfast a book was brought round in which the guests were required to sign in for lunch and dinner. The comptroller's office collated this information together with information from the invitation office and worked out how many guests would require lunch, tea or dinner that day. This information was then conveyed to the kitchens.

Ginger biscuits

This classic English recipe has been Indianised at the Rashtrapati Bhavan. Jaggery replaces brown sugar and ghee is used instead of butter or vegetable oil. The bakers also use a higher proportion of powdered ginger to flour than an English baker might, resulting in delicious sweet biscuits with a fiery kick. A Rashtrapati Bhavan staple, these biscuits are usually made in large quantities especially as they store well in air-tight containers.

Ingredients

800g jaggery • 400g desi ghee • 25g sweet soda • 2 tsp baking powder • 50g ginger powder • 1,300g plain flour

Method

Add water to the jaggery and cook to form a thin syrup.
Cool and then strain the syrup.
Add melted ghee to the syrup.
Combine flour, sweet soda, baking powder and ginger powder in a bowl and add the jaggery-ghee mixture.
Mix to form a dough and leave in the refrigerator for 30 minutes.
Roll out on a floured surface and cut out biscuit shapes.
Bake on a greased tin in the oven at 180 degrees F for 15–20 minutes.

The viceroy had to cover the cost of this endless round of entertaining out of his own salary. Southby kept a close eye on the budget. When Linlithgow's father had been governor of Australia he ended up out of pocket as a result of incessant entertaining and his son was determined that this was not going to happen to him. An acceptable cost for each meal was set. Surprisingly early morning and afternoon tea were the most expensive meals at 1 shilling 16 pence, while dinner was set at 1 shilling 2 pence. The figure for each person's expected daily food consumption was then worked out. According to the number of guests and staff a target for that week's food costs could then be calculated. A wall map in the comptroller's office was filled in showing the cost of the withdrawals of the food stores which would be necessary to make the meals for that week. If the price was kept below the target figure all was well. If not, Southby had to step in and make some adjustments. This sort of careful budgeting was normal practice in English country houses.

At Trentham Hall in Staffordshire, the steward to the duke of Sutherland kept meal books in which he recorded the cost of every meal eaten on the estate from the duke's dinners taken in the parlour to the kitchen gardener's meals eaten in the servants' hall. Even the cost of feeding the three dogs was recorded.[21] It was also common practice in English country

CLOCKWISE FROM LEFT: Uttam Bhowmick, grocery in-charge, and Vinod Kumar at work in the receiving office; Navy catering supervisor N.S. Sunil oversees the withdrawal of food items from the kitchen store by Mirza Nafiz Beg; Mohammed Qasim Qureshi, assistant baker prepares baked Alaska

houses to keep a record of the items the kitchen withdrew from the store. The British in India followed the same practice and, indeed, they kept a particularly tight check on their stores as they were convinced that Indian servants would pilfer from them if given the opportunity. At the Viceroy's House weekly menus were drawn up by the assistant comptroller of the household and approved by the comptroller and the vicereine. The kitchen staff would then apply for permission to withdraw certain foodstuffs according to the menus. They were given permission slips stating their requirements which were signed by the comptroller or his assistant.[22] An accounting system is still in place today in the Rashtrapati Bhavan. At the entrance to the kitchen corridor is the small receiving office filled with thick ledgers in which clerks keep a record of everything the cooks withdraw from the cold stores, freezers and dry goods larder.

Despite careful budgeting the cost of entertaining was high. It had always absorbed a large proportion of the viceroy's salary but the move to Lutyens' palace increased the viceroy's costs substantially. The telegram from the viceroy's military secretary to the finance department of the secretary to the government of India which discussed viceregal electricity costs raised the issue that not only did the move to the Viceroy's House require the employment of 75 additional household servants but that after just three months' residence in the new palace, the amount of coal needed to run the sophisticated heating and hot water system had already cost Rs 10,000. The house was heated by means of large water panels concealed in the floors. (Cold water could also be pumped into the panels to cool the rooms in the summer.)[23] A large coal-hungry boiler in the basement heated the water. The electricity for the kitchens cost another Rs 8,000. This was more than three times what the previous viceroy had spent in the last three years on heating hot water for baths and running the kitchens in the temporary viceregal residence in north Delhi and amounted to almost an entire month's worth of the viceregal salary.[24] The military secretary suggested that the viceroy be billed for one-third of the electricity costs and that the government should pay the remaining two-thirds. His plan was that the extra money could

be re-allocated from the viceroy's tour expenditure fund which had been reduced by about Rs 25,000 by the move from Calcutta to Delhi due to Delhi's greater proximity to Simla.[25] 'It is not [the viceroy's] fault,' he reasoned, 'that he has to live in such a much bigger house than hitherto, and if future Viceroys are to pay the total cost of the maintenance of the electric kitchens and hot water installations, it will prove very much beyond their means'.[26] The British had built their representative in India such a grand house that the running costs threatened to swallow most of his income which, as Gandhi pointed out in a letter to Irwin, at Rs 700 a day was already 5,000 times the average Indian's daily income of 2 annas a day. This, Gandhi explained, was one of the reasons why he held British rule in India to be a curse.[27]

The military secretary's telegram captured the tension inherent in the viceroy's position. Despite their upper-class backgrounds, the men who were appointed viceroy were not necessarily rich. But Disraeli's promotion of the English monarch to emperor of India in 1877 had inflated the viceroy's position. The viceroy now acted as the representative of a monarch who occupied the position of the erstwhile Mughal emperor.[28] Lords Lytton and Curzon revelled in pomp and ceremony. The ornamental ceremonial of the Raj reached its zenith with the appearance in person of King George V at the 1911 Durbar. But the glittering ostentation did not wane with the viceroys who followed. Indeed, ensconced in the stone statement of power that was the Viceroy's House the ceremony which surrounded the viceroys intensified. Lords Willingdon and Linlithgow were both intensely prestige-conscious. Peter Coats, when he was ADC to the commander-in-chief, observed that the Linlithgows preserved the 'pomp and etiquette of Akbar'.[29] Lord Wavell, who succeeded Linlithgow, was a reticent military man, less interested in ceremony. It was India's last viceroy, Lord Mountbatten, who positively gloried in the 'pageantry and vanity of imperial Delhi'.[30] He later lovingly described the outfit he wore for his investiture: 'My white full dress uniform. Orders, decorations, medals, the whole lot ... Obviously I wore the Garter. Then I wore the Star of India ... I wore the Star of the Indian Empire and then I wore the Royal Victorian Order and that made the four; that's all you're allowed to wear.'[31]

The Star of India was an order of chivalry founded by Queen Victoria in 1861 to honour the princes of India and British officers and administrators who had worked there in the Indian army and civil service. The viceroy was the grand master of the order, the medal for which was a sunburst with a light blue ring in the centre on which the order's motto was displayed. The Star of India featured in various decorations in the Viceroy's House.

FACING PAGE: Above: Group photo with the Mountbattens of the 250 staff required to run Government House [Source: Mountbatten Papers, University of Southampton archives]; Below: On occasion the viceroy and his guests ate outside in the Mughal Garden. Here the table is laid for a small party. To the left can be seen some easy chairs where the viceregal party had pre-luncheon drinks [Source: Cecil Beaton Photographs, Imperial War Museum]

LEFT: Dishes from the Star of India dinner service made for the viceroy

ABOVE: Lord and Lady Mountbatten seated on thrones in the Durbar Hall at the investiture ceremony at the Viceroy's House, 24 March 1947. They are wearing their 'orders, decorations, medals, the whole lot' [Source: Mountbatten Papers, University of Southampton archives]

LEFT: An at-home for freedom fighters in the Durbar Hall, 9 August 2015

in the house.[38] Baron Jean Pellenc thought it 'the most handsome staircase in the world'. He described how the procession of guests slowly ascending the steps to attend a viceregal ball moved in 'surging waves of light and colour … the starlit splendour of an Indian night' high above their heads.[39] The staircase was carefully designed to give the guests the feeling that they were moving into a different sphere from their own as they emerged from the dimly-lit basement level into the light and airy ambience of the king-emperor's representative.[40] A similar effect is achieved by the grand staircase at Buckingham Palace which leads guests out of the dim entry hall up steps which are deliberately shallow in order to make the staircase feel longer and more impressive. As they ascend towards the banqueting hall the amount of light filtering through to the staircase increases until the upper reaches are flooded with light from a glass dome in the ceiling.

Muriel McKnight, a guest of the civil servant Sir Frank Noyce, described how, after hanging up their coats, her party 'sailed up the marble staircase and along corridors with the gorgeous body guard on either side and along corridors to show the way'. The guests were ushered into the long drawing room where they milled about while the ADCs gradually ushered them into lines. The guests were lined up on the opposite side of the room from the house party. The ADCs quickly checked that they knew everyone's names. They would study photographs of the guests before the event and then had a few minutes to match the names to the faces they had memorised.[41] They did not always manage this seamlessly and there was something of a fuss when McKnight was at first sorted out as her host, Lady Noyce. McKnight's dinner partner, a flight lieutenant, was brought up and introduced to her and stood by her side. Then the guests of honour entered. When Muriel visited, it was the governor of Madras, Sir Stanley and his wife. They 'came in and [moved] down the whole line of guests introduced by 2 ADCs, [and] shook hands with each of us in turn'. Then the doors at the end of the room were flung open and the Willingdons appeared. They stood in the doorway while 'God Save the King' was played and then they too went down the line of guests shaking hands and receiving curtseys and bows.[42]

Butlers in the Upper Loggia where the viceroy's guests used to gather before a banquet

Once the elaborate ceremony of introductions was over, the viceroy's band played 'The Roast Beef of Old England' while everyone filed in to the banquet hall.[43] This added to the sense that one was caught up in a dramatic production as it was a tradition for English audiences at London theatres to sing this patriotic ballad at the beginning and end of a new play. It was originally composed by Henry Fielding for his *Grub-Street Opera* in 1731 but had become something of a dining anthem and was often played at important dinners in England and in military messes. When dining alone the Linlithgows were said to sing the words lustily as they went in to dinner.

The Roast Beef of Old England

Composed by Henry Fielding for the Grub Street Opera *in 1731, this song became an anthem at London theatres. It was often sung at regimental dinners and it became a tradition for the tune to be played at the Viceroy's House while the viceroy and his guests processed into dinner.*

When mighty Roast Beef was
the Englishman's food,
It ennobled our brains and enriched our blood.
Our soldiers were brave and our
courtiers were good
Oh! the Roast Beef of old England,
And old English Roast Beef!

But since we have learnt from all-vapouring France
To eat their ragouts as well as to dance,
We're fed up with nothing but vain complaisance
Oh! the Roast Beef of Old England,
And old English Roast Beef!

Our fathers of old were robust, stout, and strong,
And kept open house, with good cheer all day long,
Which made their plump tenants
rejoice in this song
Oh! The Roast Beef of old England,
And old English Roast Beef!

But now we are dwindled to, what shall I name?
A sneaking poor race, half-begotten and tame,
Who sully the honours that once shone in fame.
Oh! the Roast Beef of Old England,
And old English Roast Beef!

When good Queen Elizabeth sat on the throne,
'Ere coffee, or tea, or such slip-slops were known,
The world was in terror if e'er she did frown.
Oh! The Roast Beef of old England,
And old English Roast Beef!

In those days, if Fleets did presume on the Main,
They seldom, or never, return'd back again,
As witness, the Vaunting Armada of Spain.
Oh! The Roast Beef of Old England,
And old English Roast Beef!

Oh then we had stomachs to eat and to fight,
And when wrongs were cooking
to do ourselves right.
But now we're a . . . I could, but goodnight!
Oh! the Roast Beef of Old England,
And old English Roast Beef!

In British India even the most informal of meals was governed by the warrant of precedence. This was a book which ranked every Indian government position in descending order from the viceroy to the lowliest superintendent of jails.[44] The warrant attempted to construct for the artificial colonial society the 'natural' hierarchical order which governed society in Britain, where everyone knew his place, from the owner of the country house down to the agricultural labourer working on his estate. The warrant of precedence determined the order in which guests entered the banquet hall and where they sat at the table. British-Indian dining tables resembled those of medieval lords with the elite seated in the centre and the socially lowly seated on the outer edges. Before the event each guest was sent a printed table plan indicating the seat which they had been allocated.

The British included the princely elite in their invented social order as they regarded the princes as the natural rulers of Indian society. The British incorporated them into the imperial elite by decorating them with orders of the empire such as the Star of India and assigning them gun salutes.[45] In a letter home Peter Coats wrote, '[the Maharaja of] Bikaner is staying with us (fifteen-gun salute and don't you forget it)'.[46] Clothed in fabulous costumes and bedecked with jewels, their participation in the spectacle of British rule gave it legitimacy. Baron Pellenc was quite swept away by the glamour the princes lent proceedings. At an investiture ceremony he attended, maharajas and princesses sat behind the viceregal thrones, 'a vision of the unchanging East', dressed in the sort of glittering robes he imagined they would have worn at the durbars of the Great Mughals. Their presence gave the proceedings an air of continuity with the past, as if the British were the natural heirs of the Mughal emperors. The British added their own spurious evocations of British history. Pellenc's attention was diverted from the maharajas by heralds in Tudor-style uniforms blowing trumpets to announce the entrance of the viceroy. Pellenc was 'reminded of a scene of pageantry in a Wagnerian opera' as, to the 'slow strains of the national anthem, four officers, four ADCs and then at last, Lord and Lady Willingdon progressed into view'.[47]

The maharaja of Kapurthala who caused offence at a lunch at the Viceroy's House in January 1944 when he sat in Lord Mountbatten's place. Here he is decked out in his finery, proudly displaying the medals and orders, including the Star of India, which he had been awarded by the British [Source: Corfield Collection, Centre for South Asian Studies]

The British allowed the princes to transcend their race and join an imperial elite. As junior members of this club Indian princes and African kings, no matter the colour of their skins, rubbed shoulders with the British aristocracy. But woe betide them if they violated the code which governed relations within this upper social circle. On 14 January 1944, the maharaja of Kapurthala lunched at the Viceroy's House along with Lord Louis Mountbatten, then supreme allied commander South East Asia command. They had been allotted seats at the table in keeping with their respective positions in the warrant of precedence with Mountbatten on the vicereine's right and the Maharaja on her left. 'But,' wrote the indignant Lieutenant Colonel Humphreys in his telegram of complaint, 'on entering the dining room [the maharaja] planted himself in Lord Louis's chair. Lord Louis therefore, who came in just behind, had to sit on Her Excellency's left, faced with a table card bearing H. H.'s name.' This behaviour was considered 'extremely bad manners' and was counted a deliberate refusal on the part of the maharaja to stay both metaphorically and literally in his place. 'He will not be invited to a meal again,' continued Lieutenant Colonel Humphreys and what's more, his request that the viceroy's medical surgeon should give him a check-up should be met with the reply that the surgeon was too busy.[48]

Visitors and newcomers to India were oblivious to the fact that while 'gracious in a formal way' Raj society showed little warmth to anyone it considered a 'nobody' and outright hostility to any they considered a usurper.[49] Newcomers to the Viceroy's House were unaware that for many, precedence meant yet another excruciatingly dull dinner seated, yet again, next to an uncongenial dinner companion due to the fact that because they occupied adjacent positions in the warrant of precedence they were invariably seated next to each other. Instead, caught up in the feeling that they had been transported into a scene from the Arabian nights, visitors were thrilled by the grandeur of the setting.

As the guests filed into the banquet hall, 'all the khidmutgars ... raised both hands to their foreheads in salute'.[50] The waiters were so numerous that many visitors mistakenly thought that there was one for every guest. In fact there were 34 waiting staff employed at the Viceroy's House, one for every two or three guests when the banquet hall was at its full capacity of 104. Magnificent in their turbans, long scarlet surcoats with a bib embroidered with the viceroy's monogram, and gold-threaded scarlet belts, they imparted an air of oriental glamour to the proceedings. According to Muriel McKnight, 'the table was a dream, decorated with pale pink roses, I should think a dozen large silver vases up the centre of the table ... The table was polished [and decorated] with lace mats. The cut glass was beautiful [although] rather heavy in design'. The cutlery was ornate. When McKnight picked up her soup spoon is was so heavy she nearly dropped it.[51]

The decoration of the banquet hall was simple. The marble floor was patterned with sombre grey and white stars. Indeed, stars were a theme of the room's decoration. Each of the teak brackets running along the top of the cornice was decorated with a Star of India and the food was sometimes served on the Star of India dinner service made especially for the viceroy. Portraits of former viceroys hung along the walls. Above each of the two fireplaces on the east wall were lavish crystal and gold clocks, designed by Lutyens, and in the alcove on the southern wall shone a display of plate from the London Company of Goldsmiths and Silversmiths. The highly polished table ran the length of the austere room. A second narrow teak cornice running along the line where the ceiling cove began drew the eye upwards, accentuating its great height.

LEFT: Above: The state dining room as it was in 1931 when the house was just completed. The photograph shows how simple yet impressive the room was with its star-patterned marble floor. The second cornice above the white plaster frieze drew the eye upwards, impressing the viewer with the immense proportions of the room [Source: Centre for South Asian Studies]; Below: The main table in the state dining room set for the Mountbattens' farewell banquet. Note the Union Jack and the Indian flag displayed side by side [Source: Mountbatten Papers, University of Southampton archives]

THIS PAGE: The stars decorating each of the brackets on the cornice in the banquet hall can be seen and one of the four crystal chandeliers which hang from the ceiling. The Indian crest of the three-lion capital and the embroideries have been added since Independence and transform the state dining room into the banquet hall of the Indian President; Above the fireplace hangs one of the clocks which Lutyens designed for the state dining room

Disappointingly those guests who have left an account of their experience of dining at the Viceroy's House do not generally describe what they ate. All focus was on the pageantry of the event. On the occasion of Lord Willingdon's departure, Viola Bayley and her husband were invited to the viceregal farewell banquet for the rajas. 'I shall never forget the scene,' she wrote. The rajas were entertained in an immense shamiana in the Mughal Garden. The princes all wore so many jewels that she found in difficult not to stare. Her neighbour, the raja of Faridkhot, was charming but 'complained bitterly of the weight of the strings of uncut emeralds round his neck'.[52] The fantastic scene clearly interested her far more than anything she ate. In contrast to the contemporary celebration of food, it was considered rather bad manners in the early 20th century to comment on the food at an occasion and embarrassingly greedy to linger over sumptuous dishes. Perhaps this explains the frustrating silence on the subject. In a rare comment on the food, Cecil Beaton dismissed it as 'the inevitable banquet food'.[53] In other words, an English interpretation of French cuisine. McKnight did, however, give a description. 'We had soup, fish, some cream with grapes, chicken with peas and pot[atoes], ice soufflé, cheese savoury [shaped] like a tiny boat, crystalised fruits and sweets. Champagne ... coffee was served at the table and cigarettes.' She even described the dinner service which had a 'Copeland band of green ... and in the centre of the plate the Star of India chain with young Victoria hanging therefrom'.[54] When the now retired cook Biren Barua first came to work in the Rashtrapati Bhavan kitchens, the head cook, Deena Bandhu Barua, and senior cook, Dalim, had both begun their careers in the kitchens in the time of the viceroys. They could recall making turtle consommé, butter-soft filet mignons and quail stuffed with grapes for the viceregal banquets.[55]

The British rejected Indian food. They saw themselves as representatives of the British crown and carriers of western civilisation to India. They believed that it was therefore imperative that they should keep up appearances and project an image of themselves as fine, up-standing examples of Britishness. This meant that they sought to replicate the standards of polite society at home. This involved eating European-style meals of meat and two vegetables in heavy black broadcloth suits and tight corsets. The toughness of the meat, the fact that European vegetables were often only available in tins, the extreme discomfort of such unsuitable attire in the heat, simply served to underline their determination to preserve British standards and conventions. However, it was hard to completely eradicate Indian influences from their lives. India often made its presence felt in British food in the arena of roasts. The Indian cooks were unable to bring themselves to simply roast a plain joint of meat and would first rub it with spices. One banquet dish over which the former viceregal cooks waxed lyrical, was a leg of pork marinated for several days in beer, brandy and whisky, then rubbed with spices and 'baked to perfection'.[56]

LEFT: A plate from the dinner service used at the banquet Muriel McKnight attended in November 1931; FAR LEFT: The ruling princes' farewell banquet to Lord and Lady Linlithgow, 15 October 1943. The outgoing viceroy's farewell banquet for the maharajas was always held under a shamiana in the Mughal Garden [Source: R. Maxwell Papers, Centre for South Asian Studies]

Viceregal items from the Kitchen Museum

Trompe l'oeil dishes were a particular feature of viceregal food. Dalim used to describe how the cooks would cut up, marinate and bake a whole fish before reassembling it on the serving platter to look as though the fish was still whole. Abdul Majeed, a retired chief butler, remembered Dalim praising the confectionery cooks who excelled in the construction of elaborate trompe l'oeil creations made out of spun sugar. A popular banquet dessert was caramelised sugar strands contrived to look like tiny wicker baskets, filled with cream and fruit. The British loved a colourful table and especially admired cleverly cut fruit.[57] At Buckingham Palace the banquet table is often decorated with pre-cut pineapples reassembled to look as if they are still whole. When it is time for the dessert course, the pages surprise the guests by removing the outer shell and offering them pineapple slices.[58] It is likely that the British viceroys played the same trick on their guests. Trompe l'oeil foods had rather gone out of fashion in 1930s Britain but were still popular in British India. The confectionery cooks' sugar creations recalled Henry VIII's banquets when the tables were decorated with sugar figures of soldiers and saints and, once, an entire sugar cathedral.[59] They were also a reference to trompe l'oeil dishes made for Mughal feasts when, for example, the simple peasant dish of khichari would be manufactured out of almonds painstakingly cut to resemble rice and pistachios to resemble lentils.[60]

When he was ADC to the commander-in-chief, Peter Coats did not have a high opinion of the food produced by Linlithgow's viceregal household. He observed that it was advisable to arrive for swimming parties after dinner and complained that the food at banquets was usually stone cold.[61] This was the disadvantage of having kitchens in the basement at a distance from the banquet hall. The food was sent up from the kitchens in butler's lifts and then had to be kept in warming cupboards in the butler's pantry next to the banquet hall. The result was that the food was frequently lukewarm or, worse, cold. When Coats became Lord Wavell's comptroller the food improved. General Hartley, commander-in-chief for a short while from 1941 to 1942, and a man who 'adored his food … one day … leaned across the table in the middle of lunch to say, "Coats, I'll get you the Star of India for this salad".'[62]

The conventional banquet food served at the Viceroy's House was almost incidental to the occasion. It was the pomp and fanfare which made it remarkable. During dinner, the viceroy's personal band lightened the atmosphere by playing a selection of music. After coffee and petit fours had been served, the theatrical performance continued when a group of bagpipers from the Maratha Regiment marched twice round the room playing Scottish tunes. This tradition is also borrowed from Buckingham Palace where 12 bagpipers from the Scots or Irish Guards process around the room at the end of every state banquet.[63] The meal ended with a toast from the viceroy to the king-emperor, after which the band struck up 'God Save the King'.[64] Then the carefully choreographed process of the ladies leaving the banquet hall began. Phoebe Norton-Griffiths kept the instructions she was sent for the execution of the ceremony when she was invited to dinner with the viceroy at Government House, Calcutta on 20 December 1928. The gentlemen were requested to stand back as far as possible so that the ladies could pass in front of them. After the vicereine had stood and made her curtsey, the ladies filed out by moving clockwise around the table, stopping to curtsey opposite the viceroy, and then made their way to the drawing room.[65] At the Viceroy's House the ladies made their curtsey in the doorway.

RIGHT: Many British dishes are still made at the Rashtrapati Bhavan. Here the baker Rakesh Vaish makes British-style vol au vents as snacks for visitors

In the drawing room after dinner there was no let up from the formality. The ladies were instructed to gather into pre-assigned groups and the vicereine then moved around the room, spending a few minutes chatting to each group in turn. When the men joined the women, they all rose and went to meet the procession of men. Each guest was allotted a few minutes to talk to the viceroy, and the instructions detailed in what order they would be led up for their few minutes with the viceroy.[66] The ADCs moved the guests around, taking each person in turn up to the viceroy and moving them on if they spent too long chatting. Lord Wavell, never a sparkling conversationalist, would apparently stroke his collar when he wanted to be rescued from a particularly halting conversation.[67] There were some who found the rigid protocol irksome. Godfrey Davis, a high court judge in Karachi, took exception to being chivvied by the ADC and on one occasion when an officious aide told him that his five minutes were up he replied, 'We are having an interesting conversation and I am not moving on until we amicably end our discussion.'[68] Others found it a relief. Tom Bird was glad that lunch parties invariably broke up half an hour or less after lunch while the dinner parties would be brought tactfully to an end by the ADCs announcing, 'His Excellency is preparing to say good night', when everyone would hurriedly line up again and the viceroy and vicereine would move along the line of guests saying 'Good night!' As the couple wearily made their way to bed or very often in the case of the viceroy, back to his desk, the guests would clamber into their carriages and cars and calling, 'Jaldi! Jaldi!' to their drivers left a wake of dust on the grand driveway as they drove down Raisina Hill and back into the leafy streets of New Delhi.[69]

Notes

1. Tristram Hunt, *Ten Cities that Made an Empire* (Penguin, London, 2015), 10.
2. Ibid., 372.
3. David Cannadine, *Ornamentalism. How the British Saw Their Empire* (Allen Lane, London, 2001), 55.
4. Hicks, *India Remembered*, 50.
5. Ibid., 53.
6. Diary of Sir Francis Cannon Tudsbery, 100.
7. Narendra Singh Sarila, *Once a Prince of Sarila. Of Palaces and Tiger Hunts, of Nehrus and Mountbattens* (I.B. Tauris, London, 2008), 207.
8. Mark Bence-Jones, *Palaces of the Raj. Magnificence and Misery of the Lord Sahibs* (George Allen and Unwin, London, 1973), 203.
9. Letter, Willingdon to Hoare, 24 October 1931, Mss.Eur. E240/5, BL; Adrian Fort, *Wavell. The Life and Times of an Imperial Servant* (Jonathan Cape, London, 2009), 369.
10. Sarila, *Once a Prince of Sarila*, 244.
11. Bence-Jones, *Palaces of the Raj*, 201.
12. Details regarding the viceroy's residence (Lord Irwin), IOR/L/PO/11/9 (1925), BL, 53.
13. Letter from Lieutenant Colonel F.A. Maxwell, VC, DSO, Military Secretary to his Excellency the Viceroy, to the Secretary to the Government of India, Finance Department, 28 July 1930, National Archives, New Delhi (NAI).

The marble staircase guests now use to reach the banquet hall

14. Details regarding the viceroy's residence, 56.
15. Telegram from Viceroy, 31 August, 1929, Messages relating to furnishings, architect's fees, etc., for the Viceroy's House (1927–1931), IOR/L/PO/1/35, BL.
16. Interview with Minhaj Ali.
17. Telegram to Sir Arthur McWatters, Secretary to Government of India, Finance Department, India, 19 July 1930, from Viceregal Lodge, Simla, 1930, NAI.
18. Life in the Viceroy's House, text and prints (of photos) for a talk by Patrick Southby, ADC to the Viceroy 1938–40, Comptroller of the Viceregal Household, Patrick Henry James Southby papers, Mss. Eur. T212, IOR, BL.
19. Interview in English with Major Rajesh Kumar, Lieutenant Commander Rakesh Yadav, Major R.K. Banu Chander and Squadron Leader Yash Aryan, 18 January 2016.
20. Diary of Sir Francis Cannon Tudsbery, 90–91.
21. Pamela A. Sambrook, 'Supplies and suppliers to the country house', in *In the Country House Kitchen 1650–1900,* ed. Pamela A. Sambrook and Peter Brears (The History Press, Stroud, 2010), 197–209.
22. Life in the Viceroy's House.
23. Byron, 'New Delhi II—The interior of the Viceroy's House', 755.
24. This amounted to Rs 21,000 a month.
25. Increase of the contract grant of H.E. Viceroy by Rs 22,800, the grant for tour expenditure being reduced by Rs 25,000, and allocation of charges for the cost of running the hot water installation and the consumption of energy in the Electric Kitchen in the Viceroy's House, Viceregal Lodge, Simla, 1930 to Sir Arthur McWatters, Secretary to Government of India, Finance Department, India, 19 July 1930, NAI; The Military Secretary to His Excellency The Viceroy to the Secretary to the Government of India, Finance Department, Simla, dated 29 Aug 1930; Letter from the Military Secretary to His Excellency the Viceroy, No. 725–V.L.T dated 28 July 1930, NAI.
26. Telegram to Sir Arthur McWatters.
27. Letter from Gandhi to Irwin, 2 March 1930, Halifax Papers, Mss. Eur. C152/24, Oriental and India Office Collections, BL.

28. Cannadine, *Ornamentalism*, 51–56.
29. Peter Coats, *Of Generals and Gardens. The Autobiography of Peter Coats* (Weidenfeld and Nicolson, London, 1976), 122.
30. Hunt, *Ten Cities that Made an Empire*, 379.
31. Ibid., 380.
32. Albala, Ken, 'The historical models of food and power in European courts of the nineteenth century: an expository essay and prologue', in *Royal Taste. Food, Power and Status at the European Courts after 1789*, ed. Daniëlle de Vooght (Ashgate, Farnham, Surrey, 2011), 24.
33. Coats, *Of Generals and Gardens*, 121–2.
34. Ibid., 164.
35. Tom Bird, *Letters Home 1939–1946* (privately printed, 1996), 77.
36. Phoebe Norton-Griffiths kept some of the instructions she was sent with her invitations when she visited India in 1928–29 and stayed with the governors of Bengal and Bombay and with the viceroy at Delhi. Although some of the instructions I quote from here pertained to dinners in Government House, Calcutta, the procedure was much the same in Delhi. Instructions for dinner party guests and social procedure at Government House to meet the Viceroy and Lady Irwin at dinner at Government House, 20 December 1928, Sir Peter Norton-Griffiths Papers, Centre for South Asian Studies, Cambridge.
37. Bence-Jones, *Palaces of the Raj*, 200.
38. Life in the Viceroy's House.
39. Pellenc, *Diamonds and Dust*, 199.
40. Andreas Wohlwahsen, *Imperial Delhi. The British Capital of the Indian Empire* (Prestel, London, 2002), 108.
41. Sarila, *Once a Prince of Sarila*, 242.
42. Muriel McKnight to her family, 28 November 1931, McKnight Papers, Centre for South Asian Studies, Cambridge.
43. Instructions for dinner party guests.
44. Hunt, *Ten Cities that Made an Empire*, 376.
45. Cannadine, *Ornamentalism*, 44–45.
46. Coats, *Of Generals and Gardens*, 123.
47. Pellenc, *Diamonds and Dust*, 114–15.
48. Letter from Lt. Col. Humphreys from Viceroy's House, dated 14/1/44, Relative precedence of Lord Mountbatten to HH the Maharaja of Kapurthala, VH IOR/R/1/4/147 File 17(6)-G(S)/1943, BL.
49. Mrs Viola Bayley, Microfilm Box 7, No. 57, Centre for South Asian Studies, Cambridge, 26–27; Hall Papers, Centre for South Asian Studies, Cambridge, Vol. I, 6.
50. Letter from Enid Boon to her mother about attending an investiture at the viceroy's house, February 1939, in possession of Peter Boon.
51. Muriel McKnight to her family, 28 November 1931.
52. Mrs Viola Bayley, 25–26.
53. Cecil Beaton, *Indian Diary and Album* (OUP, Oxford, 1991), 62.
54. Muriel McKnight to her family.
55. Interview in Hindi with Biren Barua, 17 August 2014.
56. Ibid.,
57. Interview in Hindi with Abdul Majeed, 9 June 2014.
58. Jones, *For the Royal Table*, 80.
59. Eddy Stols, 'The expansion of the sugar market in Western Europe', in *Tropical Babylons. Sugar and the Making of the Atlantic World, 1450–1680*, ed. Stuart B. Schwartz, (The University of North Carolina Press, Chapel Hill & London, 2004), 237–88, 239.
60. Abdul Halim Sharar, *Lucknow. The Last Phase of an Oriental Culture*, ed. E.S. Harcourt, trans. Fakhir Hussain (Oxford University Press, Delhi, 1989), 158–62.
61. Coats, *Of Generals and Gardens,* 164.
62. Ibid.,148.
63. Jones, *For the Royal Table*, 108.
64. Diary of Sir Francis Cannon Tudsbery, 125.
65. Instructions for ladies meeting their Excellencies the Viceroy and Lady Irwin at dinner at Government House on Thursday, 20 December 1928, Sir Peter Norton-Griffiths Papers; Mrs Viola Bayley, 29; Pellenc, *Diamonds and Dust*, 98; Muriel McKnight to her family, 28 November 1931.
66. Instructions for dinner party guests.
67. Fort, *Wavell,* 371.
68. Wendy M. Davis, *Dal and Rice* (McGill-Queen's University Press, Montreal, 2009), 121.
69. Bird, *Letters Home*, 77; Beaton, *Indian Diary and Album*, 65.

The iconic photograph of Mahatma Gandhi enjoying his first ever meal at the Viceroy's House, 31 March 1947 [Source: Mountbatten Papers, University of Southampton archives]

CHAPTER 3

War and Independence

The Viceroy's House and Nationalism

Only two days after the official inauguration of New Delhi as India's capital on 15 February 1931, one of the first official visitors to the Viceroy's House was Mahatma Gandhi. Clad in a dhoti and shawl he embodied India's challenge to British rule. Even as the British moved into their new capital, built to celebrate their 'eternal' rule over India, Lord Irwin's meeting with Gandhi signalled nationalism's imminent victory. Rather than a proud statement of the permanence of British rule, Lutyens' city was, in fact, 'the tombstone of the British Raj'.[1] Gandhi's presence at the Viceroy's House indicated that the British were being forced to listen to and accommodate nationalist demands. Ever subversive of British authority, Gandhi ignored British protocol and, as he entered the palace, greeted the various members of the household staff who had contrived to be near the doorway in order to catch a glimpse of him.[2] When offered a cup of tea, having just been released from a spell in a British prison due to his salt satyagraha, he mischievously asked for a nimbu pani made with a pinch of salt.

Once Indians were admitted into the Indian civil and military services, and now that the powers of Indian politicians were increasing, the British had to find ways of fraternising with them. It was easy for the British to socialise with men like Jawaharlal Nehru, educated at Harrow and Cambridge and accustomed to mixing socially with the British.[3] It was much more difficult for them to interact with Indian politicians unfamiliar with British dining etiquette and restricted by commensal rules which meant that they did not even wish to eat with the British. When they did succeed in persuading Indian politicians to join them for dinner they were often defeated in their attempts to use the dinner table as a relaxed setting for convivial chatter. Their guests were awkward in the unfamiliar surroundings and on occasion insisted on sitting at separate tables two or three feet away from the rest of the party.[4]

British tactlessness did not help. While organising a conference in Simla, Peter Coats discovered that boef hanuman was the dish traditionally served at gala dinners at the commander-in-chief's residence. 'As half the guests were devout

Major Peter Coats, comptroller of Lord Wavell's viceregal household (on the left), talks to Lieutenant Bewley who was staying at the leave camp for officers set up at the Viceroy's House during the Second World War [Source: Cecil Beaton Photographs, Imperial War Museum]

Hindus and cannot eat beef of any kind, it shows a certain lack of tact in our predecessors at Snowden,' he wrote in a letter home. 'Hanuman,' he explained, 'is a Hindu god. It is rather like offering Catholics *Oeufs* Virgin Mary or Haddock Holy Ghost.'[5] As a way round difficult seating arrangements Coats introduced the buffet and he made sure that none of the food served was offensive to any of the guests. Everything was vegetarian and he organised two separate buffets at lunchtime. One 'suitable for Hindus' and one 'suitable for Muslims'. He was delighted when a member of Congress asked him if he was allowed to eat from both.[6]

A common compromise when the need to entertain Indians arose was to settle for tea. This was considered a more neutral meal and was generally acceptable to even the most orthodox of Indians. Gandhi's meeting with Irwin was one of many in a long campaign of chai diplomacy conducted at the Viceroy's House when British and Indian politicians tried to resolve their differences over cups of tea and snacks.

Rose petal tea

The Rashtrapati Bhavan serves rose tea at the celebrations for iftaar.

Ingredients

2 cups fresh fragrant rose petals
3 cups water
honey or sugar to taste

Method

Cut and discard the bitter white base from the petals.
Rinse them and pat them dry.
Put the petals in a saucepan and cover with the water.
Bring to a simmer for about 5 minutes
until the petals darken.
Remove from heat, strain and sweeten
with sugar or honey to taste.

Decanter tags from viceregal times now in the Kitchen Museum

The Viceroy's House and World War II

In 1939, World War II intervened in the nationalist's campaign for Independence. The war eventually brought about the demise of the Raj but life at Viceroy's House initially carried on as though nothing had changed. In the early years of the war, Linlithgow complacently surrounded himself with the usual ceremony and protocol. In December 1941 he went to Calcutta as the viceroy did every winter. The Japanese were in the process of overrunning the Malay Peninsula but the British carried on with the usual orgy of entertaining. The annual garden party was held at Government House. But it felt oddly out of place for 5,000 guests to sip tea and eat ices dressed in top hats and morning coats within range of Japanese bombers. The British mantra was that no matter the circumstances they had to keep up appearances.[7] Tom Bird who arrived in Delhi in February 1943 after having just been injured fighting in the North African desert, was acutely aware that even after three years, the war had barely touched British society in India. He wrote to his father, 'so far … I have a more or less perfect holiday all the time There is very little for me to do, and I just live in the most complete luxury eating enormous meals and doing some things I like, such as riding, squash and so on.'[8]

The grandeur of the Viceroy's House was put to work in the service of the British war effort. With the devastating Japanese victories in South East Asia, the friendship of Nationalist China suddenly become very important to the British. Nationalist leader Chiang Kai-shek and his wife were invited to Delhi in February 1941. They were entertained with all the pomp and ceremony the beleaguered Raj could muster. It was vainly hoped that Madame Kai-shek might be successful in persuading Gandhi and Nehru to mobilise support for the war. A grand banquet was held in their honour at the Viceroy's House and the ADCs rang Peter Coats in a flap 'to ask if I could hum the Chinese National Anthem down the telephone, as the Viceregal band did not know it.'[9]

In 1942, the tradition of moving up to Simla for the summer came to an end. In the conditions of wartime austerity the British could not justify the expense. Instead, the sweltering government offices were kept cool with khus-grass tatties (blinds) hung across the windows and kept damp by a small army of attendants. While lowering the temperature inside, they also gave off a pleasant aroma.[10] In 1943, Lord Wavell was appointed viceroy. He took a dim view of the previous government's mismanagement of the wartime food situation. Linlithgow's government had presided over a nationwide food crisis and a devastating famine in Bengal. Wavell insisted on the introduction of famine-relief measures and rationing in order to alleviate the general food misery. In acknowledgment of the difficult situation of a large number of hungry Indians, the number of courses at luncheon and dinner parties was reduced and the viceregal family dropped the practice of taking afternoon tea.[11] Even without a war, Wavell's personal preference was for less pomp and so he was content that wartime conditions justified the simplification of life at the Viceroy's House. The ADCs exchanged their elaborate dress uniforms for khaki suits with blue armbands. The viceroy's personal band was broken up and its members found employment elsewhere.[12] 'The Roast Beef of Old England' was no longer played as everyone filed in to dinner and Wavell did away with the tradition of bagpipers playing at the end of banquets.

Despite Wavell's more restrained regime, when war photographer Cecil Beaton visited in the first half of 1944, he noted that 'an air of leisure and prosperity' reigned over the Viceroy's House. Food was plentiful, there were servants galore, including countless ball boys at the tennis courts and plenty of old men to water the colourful herbaceous borders.[13] When he took over as Wavell's comptroller of the household, Coats did try to cut back on the number of staff but he was told that if he took them off the payroll the gardeners and sweepers, masalchies and chaprassies would simply starve. So he instituted a viceregal programme of digging for victory and put the gardeners to work in the park which was ploughed up to grow crops. The produce, which was cultivated, was sent to Delhi hospitals. The indoor staff was kept busy running a leave camp for troops which Coats established in one of the guest houses.[14]

Delhi official society remained shamefully cut off from the realities of the war. At one viceregal dinner party, Beaton listened to an elderly Indian gentleman complaining that first quality rice was only obtainable on the black market. Next to him an elegant Englishwoman remarked that her greatest irritation was the difficulty of buying a bottle of whisky.[15] Bird turned down Wavell's offer to accompany him to the Viceroy's House. 'I should be ashamed to be there while there is a war on,' he explained in a letter to his mother, 'and dread to think what I should be [like] in a year.'[16] Not only were the Delhi elite oblivious to the hardship of the ordinary Indians that surrounded them, they were also insulated from the shortages and discomfort endured by their compatriots back in Britain. When Edwina Mountbatten arrived at the Viceroy's House in March 1947 she asked for some food to give her dog. A cooked breast of chicken duly arrived on a silver salver. Not having seen chicken for quite some time in wartime Britain where poultry was scarce, Edwina did not give it to her dog but locked herself in the bathroom and ate it.[17] Contemplating his return to England in 1947, Peter Coats wondered whether his English friends would resent 'the fact that I had hardly known the Blitz, had hardly seen a ration book, and had never eaten spam or snoek?'[18]

The end of the war was marked at the Viceroy's House by a characteristically extravagant celebratory party. Coats organised it with his usual panache. Using large oil drums filled with torn up and dampened old office files he created four '*feux de joie*' (celebratory bonfires) on the roof of the house. The towering columns of smoke were 'cheap but spectacular'. Floodlit in red, white and blue they could be seen for miles. He also turned on the roof fountains for the occasion with similarly spectacular effect but disastrous consequences as the water brought down the ceilings in three of the state bedrooms. Symbolising the new state of political affairs in India, the Mughal Garden was filled with British, American and Australian soldiers from the leave camps, rubbing shoulders with dhoti-clad Indian politicians, maharajas in rubies and British memsahibs in thin cotton dresses. Indian whisky and beer lubricated the proceedings and the crowd were entertained by the combination of an Indian dancer on a floodlit stage, Indian sitar music and an English band.[19]

Rajkumari Amrit Kaur, the health minister and the first woman in the cabinet, seated between the outgoing, Lord Mountbatten and incoming, C. Rajagopalachari, governor generals of India at the farewell banquet of 20 June 1948 [Source: Mountbatten Papers, University of Southampton archives]

The Viceroy's House and Independence

The imprisonment of Congress leaders for most of the war brought chai diplomacy to a temporary halt. But by the end of the war it was clear that the days of British rule in India were numbered. The Viceroy's House became the setting for many of the negotiations which eventually led to Indian Independence. Gandhi started visiting the viceroy again and Coats recalled what an odd picture he and Lady Wavell made seated in deep sofas in her chintzy sitting room. 'Lady Wavell large and motherly in a printed silk dress, and the Mahatma to all intents and purposes naked except for a loin-cloth.'[20] Indian politicians proved adept at using British-style tea parties for their own ends. By 1946, an interim government run by Nehru and Sardar Vallabhbhai Patel had been established. In theory Lord Wavell presided over the interim government but whenever they were supposed to meet Nehru made sure that the Indian politicians assembled for tea beforehand. Wavell was frustrated that he was never invited to these 'tea-party cabinets' where the real business was done and policy was decided before the official meeting.[21] Unable to break the deadlock of independence negotiations, Wavell was recalled from India in the spring of 1947.

Mountbatten, the last viceroy of India, was quite different from the notoriously reserved Wavell. He embarked on a charm offensive, relentlessly inviting Indians from all walks of life to the Viceroy's House. In his April personal report to London he noted, 'we have had two garden parties and have about three luncheon parties of 30, and larger dinners each week, at which I have made it a rule that not less than 50 per cent of those present must be Indians.'[22] Mountbatten's wife, Edwina, and his daughter, Pamela, helped by socialising with the Indian ladies on these occasions.[23] Gandhi became an even more frequent visitor. One morning he even conceded to eat in the Englishman's presence and had his breakfast in the gardens. Mountbatten was persuaded to try a spoonful of the goat's curds which he pronounced 'the most disgusting green porridge that he'd ever had'.[24]

An affectionate relationship developed between Nehru and both the Mountbattens. Mountbatten's ADC, Narendra Singh Sarila, noted in his diary that Nehru 'was chummy with Their Excellencies. Came for two minutes, stayed for 2 hours'.[25] Nehru's niece described how Mountbatten would drop in casually at Nehru's house and eat strawberry ice cream in the garden.[26] To some, the friendship was politically improper, especially as it led the leaders of India's other political parties to feel that it influenced British political decisions.[27]

Nevertheless, Mountbatten carried out his government's instructions, with an almost unseemly haste and India gained its Independence on 15 August 1947. After Independence, the Mountbattens stayed on at the house for another year. But on 20 June 1948, only 18 years after Irwin had moved into Lutyens' testament to enduring British rule in India, a special banquet was held to bid farewell to its last British inhabitants.

Notes

1. *The Yorkshire Post*, 11 February 1931, cited by Hunt, *Ten Cities that Made an Empire*, 347.
2. Bence-Jones, *Palaces of the Raj*, 202.
3. Stanley Wolpert, *Nehru. A Tryst with Destiny* (OUP, Oxford, 1996), 239.
4. Interview in English with Tom A. Bird, 4 June 2015.
5. Coats, *Of Generals and Gardens*, 123–4.
6. Ibid., 252.
7. Ibid., 145.
8. Bird, *Letters Home*, 82.
9. Coats, *Of Generals and Gardens,* 149.
10. Ibid., 164.
11. Bence-Jones, *Palaces of the Raj*, 205.
12. 8 May 1948, Government House, New Delhi, C. Rajagopalchari Papers (vinst) Sas. File 76, 12, Records Room, Rashtrapati Bhavan.
13. Beaton, *Indian Diary and Album*, 15.
14. Coats, *Of Generals and Gardeners*, 211.
15. Beaton, *Indian Diary and Album*, 63.
16. Bird, *Letters Home*, 96.
17. Hicks. *India Remembered*, 19.
18. Coats, *Of Generals and Gardens*, 259.
19. Ibid., 248–9.
20. Ibid., 254.
21. Patrick French, 'Goat's curd, Mr Viceroy?', *The Week*, 15 February 2015.
22. Viceroy's Personal Report No. 3 (17 April 1947), IOR/L/PO/6/123, 42 50, BL.
23. Hicks, *India Remembered*, 55.
24. Ibid., 69, 70.
25. Sarila, *Once a Prince,* 253.
26. French, 'Goat's curd, Mr Viceroy?'
27. H.M. Close, *Attlee, Wavell and the Transfer of Power* (National Book Foundation, Islamabad, 1997), 55.

RIGHT: Staff hurry to prepare the Durbar Hall for an indoor at-home after it rained on the outdoor venue; TOP: Captain Prashant Singh, the comptroller, checks the arrangements for a banquet BELOW: Manwar Singh Rawat, the chief butler, and Sabir Ali, a butler, check the arrangements for a luncheon

ABOVE: The butlers Sabir Ali and Samee Alam Khan pour fresh fruit juice before guests arrive to lunch

LEFT: Butlers at work

Eve Curie's fantasy made true. Governor General Rajagopalachari hosts Lady Mountbatten to tea at Government House, 15 February 1949 [Source: Rashtrapati Bhavan Photo Section]

CHAPTER 4

DINING WITH THE PRESIDENT

THE VICEROY'S HOUSE BECOMES THE RASHTRAPATI BHAVAN

When the American journalist Eve Curie was asked to lunch at the Viceroy's House in 1942, uppermost in her mind was the news that Sir Stafford Cripps was on his way to India with instructions from the war cabinet to offer India dominion status or even independence in return for India's full support during the war. Curie found that she could not help thinking 'irreverent thoughts … Should I come back there one day to see Gandhi sipping his daily ration of goat milk? To whom would we curtsy then? Would the delightful Cambridge-educated Nehru be there, swimming in the pool, playing tennis, or holding joint audiences with his ferocious opponent of the Moslem League, Mr Jinnah?'[1] At the time she dismissed these thoughts as fantasy. But if Curie had returned only six years later she would have found a dhoti-clad, strict vegetarian had indeed taken up residence at the Viceroy's House. When Lord Mountbatten stood down as governor general in June 1948, he was replaced by C. Rajagopalachari, the first and only Indian governor general.

A south Indian Brahmin who had been a close associate of Gandhi and a fellow freedom-fighter, Governor General Rajagopalachari at first felt uncomfortable at the prospect of moving into the ostentatious palace. But the Indian Republic had inherited New Delhi as its capital and C. Rajagopalachari was persuaded by Mountbatten and Nehru that the palace was the most suitable venue to host the dignitaries who would surely visit the newborn nation. The new governor general did make changes to tone down the grandeur and luxury that had attended the personal life of the viceroy. He rejected the viceroy's private apartments and chose instead to live in the modest suite of four rooms which had housed Lady Mountbatten's lady-in-waiting. This has remained the president's personal suite ever since.

When he was not attending state functions Governor General Rajagopalachari preferred to eat food prepared by his widowed daughter rather than the more formal meals prepared in the basement kitchens. He therefore installed a private kitchen in his apartment. All the presidents since then, except A.P.J. Abdul Kalam, have followed in his footsteps, and have maintained a private kitchen. A bachelor, President Kalam preferred to eat from the main kitchen rather than employ a retinue of kitchen staff to cater just for him. Sometimes the presidents brought their own cooks to staff their private household and others seconded cooks from the main kitchens and butlers from the household. These members of the staff developed special relationships with the presidents they served and often felt a particular affection for them.[2] Minhaj

Ali, now a senior cook in the main kitchens, worked in the presidents' private kitchen in the 1970s and '80s when he was a cook's mate. He would assist the cook and sometimes serve the president. He enjoyed working for President Neelam Sanjiva Reddy because he so enjoyed his food and he was known fondly as 'nawanmunda' by President Giani Zail Singh as he made such delicious bottle gourd cooked in milk.[3]

Rajendra Prasad replaced Governor General Rajagopalachari as India's first president on 26 January 1950. He adopted a similarly modest Gandhian presidential style. Every morning he performed puja and then, in true Gandhian fashion, spun on his charkha while his assistant, Gayanwati Darbar, read to him.[4] No doubt he sipped on goat's milk from time to time. His successor, Sarvepalli Radhakrishnan was a learned philosopher and scholar who led a similarly unpretentious personal life and, like his predecessors, was also a strict vegetarian. When she speculated on its future inhabitants, Curie had concluded that anyone other than an Englishman would look ridiculous amidst the pompousness of the house. But she was wrong. She would have been impressed by the figures of these men who walked Lutyens' long corridors of power, dignified in their simple white Indian attire.[5]

In the public areas Governor General Rajagopalachari took over the apparatus of the Viceroy's House more or less wholesale. Having inherited everything from the British—the building, the staff, the furniture, the linen and the crockery—it was difficult to completely throw off the past. Almost all the household staff from viceregal times continued to work at the house and with the staff the Indian state inherited an army thoroughly trained in the maintenance of Raj protocol and etiquette. The staff acted as repositories of the house traditions. Each viceroy or president only inhabited the palace for a short while. Their official staff came and went with them, but the household staff remained. Every butler knew the correct way to lay a banquet table so that each guest's place setting took up exactly 46 centimetres. The cooks were masters of French-style European banquet food. The khidmatgars were adept at butler service, always offering the dishes on the guest's left so that they could serve themselves using their right hand. Each new member of staff was carefully inducted into the etiquette of the palace. Karimullah, the chief butler, who has been working at the Rashtrapati Bhavan for 38 years, explained that the young butlers looked up to their seniors, just as the junior cooks and cook's mates looked up to the head cooks. In this way the butlers and the cooks learned their craft from their seniors and the viceregal traditions were passed on down the generations. The system constantly reproduced itself. The Rashtrapati Bhavan could not help but inherit some of the traditions of the Viceroy's House.[6]

Each new incumbent feels the weight of the Rashtrapati Bhavan tradition. President Prasad was aware of the irony that he felt he was more intensely observed in the Rashtrapati Bhavan than he had been as a prisoner of the British.[7] Intense scrutiny was accompanied

Manwar Singh Rawat, chief butler; Kundan Singh, head butler, and Muquaddar Hussain, butler, enjoy a quiet moment in the Upper Loggia

by the expectation that the president should behave in a particular way. President R. Venkataraman described how he 'constantly came across the established view of the staff about how a President should function. Whenever I tried to make an implicit or explicit claim to be myself and not only the President, there were often objections from the staff.'[8] In this way the weight of tradition pressed down on and shaped each president's behaviour. It was difficult to break with the traditions or reject protocols in which the staff firmly believed. Besides, India's politicians found themselves operating in a world of diplomacy where certain standards were expected and India did not want to be seen to be unable to compete.

Governor General Rajagopalachari did make one very important symbolic change. He replaced the British monogram of a crown, which the servants wore on the bibs of their uniforms, with the three-lion capital which had been adopted as the new Republic's symbol.[9] This same monogram is still in use today. It also decorates the Rashtrapati Bhavan's crockery and glassware and it gives patriotic Indian visitors a frisson of pleasure to eat and drink from utensils emblazoned with this symbol of the Republic.[10]

FAR LEFT: Teacups laid out in readiness for the guests at a ceremony for India's freedom fighters on 9 August 2015. Each cup is emblazoned with India's monogram of the three-lion capital

LEFT: Anil, a butler with the three-lion capital monogram displayed on his uniform

A banquet at the Rashtrapati Bhavan in the early years of the Indian Republic. [Source: private collection]

The Rashtrapati Bhavan is made Indian

During the 1950s and 60s, while India was finding her place in the world, the Rashtrapati Bhavan was visited by numerous foreign heads of state. The Soviet Union's premier and the first secretary of the Communist party, Nikolai Bulganin and Nikita Khrushchev, made the first official Russian visit to India in 1955 and Zhou En-lai the Chinese premier paid a visit in 1960. Queen Elizabeth II and the heads of newly independent African countries Zaire, Zambia and Tanzania came to celebrate India's Independence on different Republic Days. President Prasad was reportedly gloomy about the prospect of atheist communists eating meat and drinking alcohol in the guest suite where a special room, supplied with alcoholic beverages, had been set up for the Russians.[11] The staff, however, enjoyed these visits. 'Those days were fun,' reminisced Abdul Majeed, a retired butler who worked at the house in the early years of the presidency. 'All heads of states used to stay here in [the] Dwarka suite and were served all the meals by us.'[12] The Russian delegation did their best not to offend Indian sensibilities by avoiding the drinks room but they were apparently hearty eaters and in between formal meals would send up for extras such as omelettes and sandwiches.[13] While the tips were marvellous, the butlers derived most of their satisfaction from the pride they took in working for the representative of their newly independent nation.

The Indian state gradually grew into and made its own the traditions and protocol that it had inherited from the Raj. In the early days the portraits of past viceroys still hung on the walls of the banquet hall.[14] Gradually these were moved out of the room and replaced by paintings of India's former presidents. At first, the food served at the Rashtrapati Bhavan continued to be Anglicised-French in style, as it had been during the tenure of the viceroy. French food was

Pomme Croquettes

A typically Anglo-Indian recipe which the Rashtrapati Bhavan kitchens still make.

Ingredients

400g potatoes * salt * pepper * pinch of nutmeg
1 egg yolk * a knob of butter * 1 tsp plain flour
1 whole egg * a little milk * 150g breadcrumbs
oil for cooking

Method

Wash, peel and boil potatoes.
Mash them with salt pepper, nutmeg an egg yolk and a knob of butter until they have a smooth and creamy consistency.
Mix together plain flour, salt, pepper, a whole egg and a little milk until the mixture becomes slightly sticky to make a batter. Divide the potato mixture into golf-ball size balls and roll into cylinders.
Dip in the batter and then roll in bread crumbs.
Heat cooking oil in a kadhai and deep fry the potato croquettes individually until golden brown.

the international food of state occasions, synonymous with fine dining across the world. When Franklin Delano Roosevelt served George VI hot dogs at a picnic this was a bold statement of national pride. But relations between America and Britain were amiable and the circumstances were relaxed.[15] If the Indian governor general or president had served Indian food at a banquet it might have seemed gauche, as if the Indians were not *au fait* with international standards. And so European food dominated at the early Indian state occasions.

On 24 January 1950, the assembled company at the banquet for President Sukarno described by Indrani Jagjivan Ram at the beginning of this book, were served cream of spinach soup followed by fillet de pomfret frit or fried fish with sauce tartare. This was a typically Anglo-Indian dish, ubiquitous on British dining tables throughout the subcontinent through the long years of British rule. While Indrani was internally rolling her eyes and quietly wondering whether India would ever throw off the habits of the British, her husband was almost certainly pleased. Probably as a result of sharing so many meals with the British, he had acquired a taste for fried fish and tartare sauce and would often order it to accompany family meals, even when the rest of the menu was solidly Indian.[16]

Instead of fried fish the vegetarian option for this course was the equally Anglo-Indian 'vegetable cutlets' made of

A place setting at the banquet table

CLOCKWISE FROM ABOVE: President Rajendra Prasad hosts a thali lunch for Bhagwan Dass and Sir M. Visveswaray, 7 August 1955 [Source: Rashtrapati Bhavan Photo Section]; President S. Radhakrishnan gives a speech at a banquet in honour of the Mexican president on 6 October 1962. The food was still solidly European in style [Source: Rashtrapati Bhavan Photo Section]; President Prasad raises a toast to K.E. Voroshilov, Chairman of the Presidium of the Supreme Soviet of the USSR, on 20 January 1960. Despite President Prasad's objections, the Rashtrapati Bhavan has maintained the tradition of toasting the guest of honour [Source: Rashtrapati Bhavan Photo Section]

vegetables mashed and then shaped to look like chops and fried. The main course was caneton à la diable, peas with cauliflower and roast potatoes. The duck in a piquant mustard and cayenne sauce was a touch of French sophistication. The alternative vegetarian main course was the only part of the meal which gave away the fact that the dinner was taking place in India. Indrani was served aloo dum, cauliflower curry, raita, papad and chutney. The red rose indicating her vegetarian preferences was an Indian innovation. During the British period, the vegetarian and other food preferences of the guests were indicated to the butlers by ribbons tied to the backs of the chairs. Just as both the vegetarian and non-vegetarian meal began with a very British soup, they both ended with the same very British dessert, pommes Chantilly or stewed apples decorated with swirls of cream.

The regimental band did introduce an Indian note to the banquet by playing Hindustani songs during the dinner and one striking change from the viceregal times was that wines and spirits were banished from the table. Indeed, alcohol was banished from the Rashtrapati Bhavan other than in the guests' Dwarka suite. Alcohol had offended Gandhi and it was now officially abjured by the Indian state. The traditional toast was drunk with sherbet rather than champagne. Even then President Prasad objected to this tradition. He complained to his secretary, 'I have to propose the toast at every formal banquet, although we do not drink any wine.' He found the 'custom … really objectionable, as it contemplates drinking although we may not resort to it.' Listening to All India Radio one evening he learned that at a state banquet for the king of Saudi Arabia, President Eisenhower had not proposed a toast. He argued that the Rashtrapati Bhavan should follow this example and find an Indian substitute. But his suggestion was rejected on the grounds that the toast was a recognised international custom. The Indian state was still too new to confidently reject anything which was part of an international code of conduct. Toasts are still made at Rashtrapati Bhavan banquets as an innocuous gesture of friendship, although they are left out of banquets for Arabian heads of states who also abstain from alcohol.[17]

If President Prasad failed to excise the toast from the banquet he did manage to introduce the Indian thali with all its accompaniments to the Rashtrapati Bhavan banquet hall. He reported that foreign guests appreciated this Indian system of serving a meal. But even President Prasad who instinctively resisted the European form of a meal, had to admit that thali banquets were wasteful.[18] Every thali was supplied with a generous helping of each dish whereas butler service ensured that guests only served themselves with the dishes they liked and the quantity of food that they wanted to eat. Banquet guests tend to eat little and so a lot of food was thrown away after thali meals. The Rashtrapati Bhavan reverted to the European-style banquet with butler service for grand occasions. Thalis were served at all-Indian gatherings such as the governors' conference and more intimate dinners. Today the Rashtrapati Bhavan serves thalis with dishes from many different regions for particular ceremonies such as the swearing in of a new prime minister or at the meeting of South Asian heads of state.[19] Nevertheless, waste seems to have been a problem even at the European-style banquets in the early years. A dhaba at the New Delhi Gole Market is said to have offered leftovers from the Rashtrapati Bhavan kitchens on its menu blackboard as 'Rashtrapati Bhavan ka khana'.[20]

The first course at viceregal banquets was always soup and the Rashtrapati Bhavan has remained faithful to this tradition. Although soup is a decidedly un-Indian dish, the cooks have become expert in preparing French cordon bleu soups such as crème nivernaise (onion) or consommé royal (clear vegetable). In 1990 Biren Barua made such delicious celery soup for Yasser Arafat that the Palestinian president complemented him personally.[21] The second course at the Rashtrapati Bhavan is invariably fish. In the 1950s and 60s the fish dishes were old Raj favourites such as bekti paupette or baked pomfret. Sureshwar Sawhney, who was ADC to President Prasad, recalled the food at that time was fabulous.[22]

When Minhaj Ali joined the kitchens in 1974 he recalled that hardly any Indian food was prepared there, it was virtually all continental. In fact, when the cooks wanted to make food for themselves they had to bring in their own masala and rice. In October 1962 when the president of Mexico visited India he was served chicken in an Italian style.

The sweets produced by the halwai kitchen are favourites with the Rashtrapati Bhavan staff and visitors alike. Here Kailash Yadav and Raja Ram, halwais, are making imarti and jalebi, Gopal Chandra Bharadwaj is making saffron sauce, and Suresh Kumar, the cook mate, is mixing maawa to make barfi. Kailash replaced Haider Ali when he moved into the main kitchens. He now concentrates on training his assistants to take his place when he retires

But just as the viceregal portraits were slowly edged out of the banquet hall, so European-style meat dishes were gradually replaced by Indian dishes. In March 1963, the meal for the vice president of Cyprus began with almond soup followed by fried prawns with tartare sauce and ended with a European-style fruit gateau. But the main course was a veritable Indian feast of nargisi kofta and raisina pulao, tandoori chicken, aloo masala, chaman matar and naan bread.[23] By the time President Reddy came to reside at the Rashtrapati Bhavan in July 1977, Indian food was firmly established on the menu. However, following the old British practice of only allowing Indian food on to the breakfast and lunch tables, but never the dinner table, throughout the 1980s the ADCs were only served Indian food at lunch time. Their breakfast and main meal in the evening were always continental.

The cheerful amateurism of the 1950s was replaced in the 1960s by a determined programme of Indianisation. Nehru was very keen to Indianise the protocol which surrounded the Indian president and enlisted the help of his daughter, Indira Gandhi. She and Tara Ali Baig, the wife of the chief of protocol, did away with many of the old viceregal practices. Bouquets were replaced with garlands and at state banquets the ladies were no longer asked to withdraw after dessert. They had ceased to curtsey on leaving the banquet hall with the departure of Lord Mountbatten.[24] As prime minister, Indira Gandhi continued to keep a close eye on the menus and her office liaised with the president's to decide on the food for every event.[25]

Zill-e-Darvesh

This is Haider Ali's personal recipe for the dish which he invented when he was appointed as a halwai in the Rashtrapati Bhavan kitchens.

Ingredients

100g powdered almonds * 200g grated reduced milk (khoya) * 200g sugar * ¼ tsp nutmeg powder * ¼ tsp mace powder * 200g melted desi ghee * ½g saffron

For the garnish

2 gold leaves * 20g almond slivers * 20g pistachio slivers

Method

In a pan roast the grated khoya with the almond powder, sugar, mace and nutmeg powders and the saffron. Once the mixture has blended together, add the melted desi ghee, and fry on low heat for some time, stirring all the while. When the ghee has been fully absorbed, remove and cool. The mixture should have the consistency of fudge. Spread the mixture in a tray and let it cool. Cover the mixture with gold leaf, garnish with almonds and pistachio slivers. Cut into small pieces and serve.

Indian puddings such as almond kheer and mango ice cream began to replace British trifles and custard creams.[26] In the late 1960s, the Rashtrapati Bhavan discovered that it had a master of Indian sweet cookery working in the kitchens of its guesthouse. Haider Ali began his career at the palace as a butler in the chandikhana polishing the silver and brassware, a position he acquired through his father-in-law who was one of the president's drivers. Haider also had a sweet shop and catering business in old Delhi. It was after he had cooked a fantastic banquet for the president's military secretary, Major General R.L. Chopra, that he was moved to the main kitchens. Up until now the Rashtrapati Bhavan had bought any Indian sweets it required from Delhi's various high-class bakeries and sweets shops such as Gaylord's or Wengers in Connaught Place, Nathu Sweets at Bengali Market or Sandesh House on Chandni Chowk. But after the head cook had tasted the Indian sweets Haider made at his trial he was appointed the Rashtrapati Bhavan's halwai. Soon he was making halwa, zauq-e-shahi, barfi, imarti and makhanbada as Indian snacks and desserts for the banquets. He also made kulfis and ice creams with a hand machine in the kitchens. His sweets were so popular that he was asked to bake for staff wedding parties.[27]

After dinner on 20 January 1960 the guests are entertained by Indian dancers, including Indrani Rahman [Source: Rashtrapati Bhavan Photo Section]

In viceregal times the naval jazz band often played after dinner. Presidential after-dinner entertainments celebrated Indian culture. Indian dancers were frequently invited to the Rashtrapati Bhavan to perform for guests.[28] In the 1980s President Venkataraman renovated the basement cinema which had been a favourite haunt of the viceroys. After dinner the viceregal party would retire to the basement to watch a film. Lord Wavell recounted how when Lord Mountbatten (then supreme allied commander South East Asia command) came to dine at the Viceroy's House in 1943, 'we had a cinema *Casablanca*, a typical film story of the sentimental-thriller type'. Mountbatten was horrified to find that Wavell, who was not a great film fan, was 'neither touched nor thrilled' and asked whether he at least liked musical films with 'cheerful songs and dancing'. Lord Wavell feared that his reply that he was not musical had given the impression that he was 'a cheerless kill-joy'.[29] When Mountbatten himself became viceroy, his love of films was evident. Dinner guests would 'invariably [be invited to] watch a film, with brandy and cigars served ... during the show'.[30] Governor General Rajagopalachari continued with the viceregal tradition but when he invited the Rashtrapati Bhavan staff to a screening of a movie he included all the staff from the comptroller of the household to the most junior peon. Dooj Prakash, who was then an office boy, was included in the invitation to watch the movie and, without discrimination, the staff were offered chairs to sit on. This was an overt rejection of British rules which only allowed men of rank to sit in the presence of British officers. Dooj recalled that some of the British officers and staff walked out of the hall. But the days when the British set the agenda at the Rashtrapati Bhavan were now over. Dooj, who had begun his working life at the palace as a ball boy on the viceregal tennis courts, observed with satisfaction that all the ADCs were now Indian and the entire atmosphere of government had 'turned Indian'.[31]

President Venkataraman revived the cinema and would occasionally screen an award-winning film. He also organised a series of music concerts and dance performances. A list of permanent invitees was drawn up, among them the prime minister and various politicians, all of whom found it difficult to attend public performances. According to President Venkataraman they all eagerly looked forward to these cultural evenings.[32]

Indian dancers led by Birju Maharaj entertain President Françoise Mitterrand of France on 27 November 1982 [Source: Rashtrapati Bhavan Photo Section]

The Rashtrapati Bhavan as the President's Home

The Rashtrapati Bhavan kitchens are those of India's grandest home rather than of a hotel. However, recent presidents have concerned themselves with improving the professional standards of the kitchen and waiting staff. In the early years of the presidency, the cooks were recruited from among the sons of the household staff. Basheer Ahmed's father worked in the Rashtrapati Bhavan's laundry and Basheer was born and brought up on the estate. After his father retired in 1984, he was taken on as a cook's mate in the kitchens. He had received no formal training but learned from watching the senior cooks.[33] The excellence of Basheer's galouti kebabs, which have just the right blend of aromatic spices, attests to the success of this method of training the cooks. However, in the 1990s, the cooks began to widen their horizons and were sent for training weeks at Delhi's top hotels. By watching the hotel chefs they learned new culinary techniques and recipes. At the banquet for the Aga Khan on 14 November 1992, the cooks proudly showed off their dal bukhara, a slow-cooked black lentil dish which they had learned to cook at the Maurya Hotel. In the 1950s Nehru set up the ITDC and the corporation's first hotel, the Ashoka, was built to accommodate the large delegations that accompanied state visitors. By shadowing the chefs at the Ashoka, the Rashtrapati Bhavan cooks have honed their soup and salad-making skills.[34] The butlers also receive training in the hotels and President A.P.J. Abdul Kalam, determined that the table service at the Rashtrapati Bhavan should be every bit as elegant and efficient as that at Buckingham Palace, sent members of the household to be trained at the Leela Palace Hotel in Mumbai by a former Buckingham Palace butler.[35]

When the kitchens were installed in the 1920s they may have been the most modern in the empire but they have needed updating several times since then. Minhaj recalled that when he started working in 1974, the kitchens were hot and uncomfortable with only fans to provide a little relief for the sweltering staff who used to work in their vests

The army band entertains guests on 15 August 2015

and shorts. He was envious of the bakers whose pastries and cakes had to be made away from the intense heat of the stoves though Razi Haider could only recall there being one ceiling fan to cool the bakers down. Refrigeration was rudimentary in those days and the kitchens relied on an ice plant to provide ice for the wooden icebox in which they stored the meat.[36] The cooks' mates had to grind the spices by hand on grinding stones and even more arduously, lentils and rice to make idli and dosa batter.[37] In the early days the cooks used charcoal-fuelled bhattis. In President Singh's time (1982–87) gas stoves were introduced along with better refrigeration facilities but much of the cooking still had to be done on hot plates. The bakers had to control the heat of their ovens with mercury thermometers.[38] It was not until President Kalam's (2002–07) tenure that it was decided that the kitchens were in need of a thorough overhaul. Plans were put in place for the installation of a gas pipe to supply the stoves and for modern electric tandoor ovens and large temperature-regulated electric ovens to be installed in the bakery. It was decided to equip the cooks and bakers, who had until now done everything by hand, with steamers, slicers, grinders, mixers and kneaders and a belt to roll out cookie dough and pastry. The modernisation was still only in the planning stages when President Kalam left office, but President Patil (2007–12), pleased to improve working conditions for her staff who produced such splendid food in trying conditions, made sure that the plans were realised. By 2009 the cooks were equipped with a thoroughly modern air-conditioned kitchen.

Every one of the palace's 19 VIP occupants has put his or her own stamp on the Rashtrapati Bhavan. Each one treated the house as a home, not a museum. Lutyens planned everything down to the last detail. Each carpet was designed for a specific room and had the name of the room embroidered on the backing. Every piece of furniture was designed so that it fitted in a particular alcove and had a numbered brass plate attached to it to show to which room it belonged.[39] But each new inhabitant has made alterations and moved the furnishings around. Major Meysey Clive, ADC to Lord Willingdon, noted down what he considered to be Lady Willingdon's decorating crimes in a small notebook. Among them was the vulgar planting of canna lilies in the Mughal Garden and the installation of red lights at the four corners of the dome to signify whether the viceroy was at home. Worse still was the re-siting of a 'monstrous' statue from the

Burmese pavilion at the 1911 Durbar in the kitchen court, probably what is now the south court, at a cost of Rs 2,000.[40] Lady Linlithgow brought Lutyens back to the palace to sort out her predecessor's muddle. But a succession of Indian presidents has closed up rooms, moved the furniture around and used the rooms in unusual ways. President Fakhruddin Ali Ahmed is supposed to have turned the Long Drawing Room into a badminton court. In the 1960s Anjolie Ela Menon's father was surgeon to the president. One day on an inspection tour of the house and grounds he discovered 'six cows tethered to the gilded taps and fixtures in one of the grand bathrooms, steadily munching from the large marble bathtub. However, there was little that he could do because he was informed that these constituted the First Lady's personal herd and that she liked to milk them herself.'[41] The president's herd obviously had something of a reputation as in July 1967 President Zakir Husain received a request from a hospital in Gurgaon for a British bred cow. The hospital was disappointed as the military secretary informed them that the president did not own any cows of a British breed. He did however give a calf to a school in Meerut in the September of that year on the condition that he might receive in return its first female offspring.[42]

President K.R. Narayanan, who loved music, reinstated the naval jazz band which was dispersed during the Second World War.[43] President Patil, looking for a unique way to end state dinners, revived the tradition of the bagpiper to mark the end of a state banquet. Once the coffee and petit fours had been consumed, a piper would march around the room playing until he came to a stop behind the chief guest to announce that the dinner was over.[44] The bagpiper has since been dropped on the grounds that the sound was excruciatingly loud. At some point the white plaster frieze round the top of the banquet hall was decorated with crossed scimitars. There is no sign of them in viceregal photographs so these must have been installed soon after the British had departed. President Patil was offended by the martial air this gave the room. She thought it inappropriate in a dining room and had them replaced with embroideries which echo the shapes of the various Indian states.

OVERLEAF: The portrait of Mahatma Gandhi is flanked by the flags of India and France on the occasion of the banquet for the French president, François Hollande

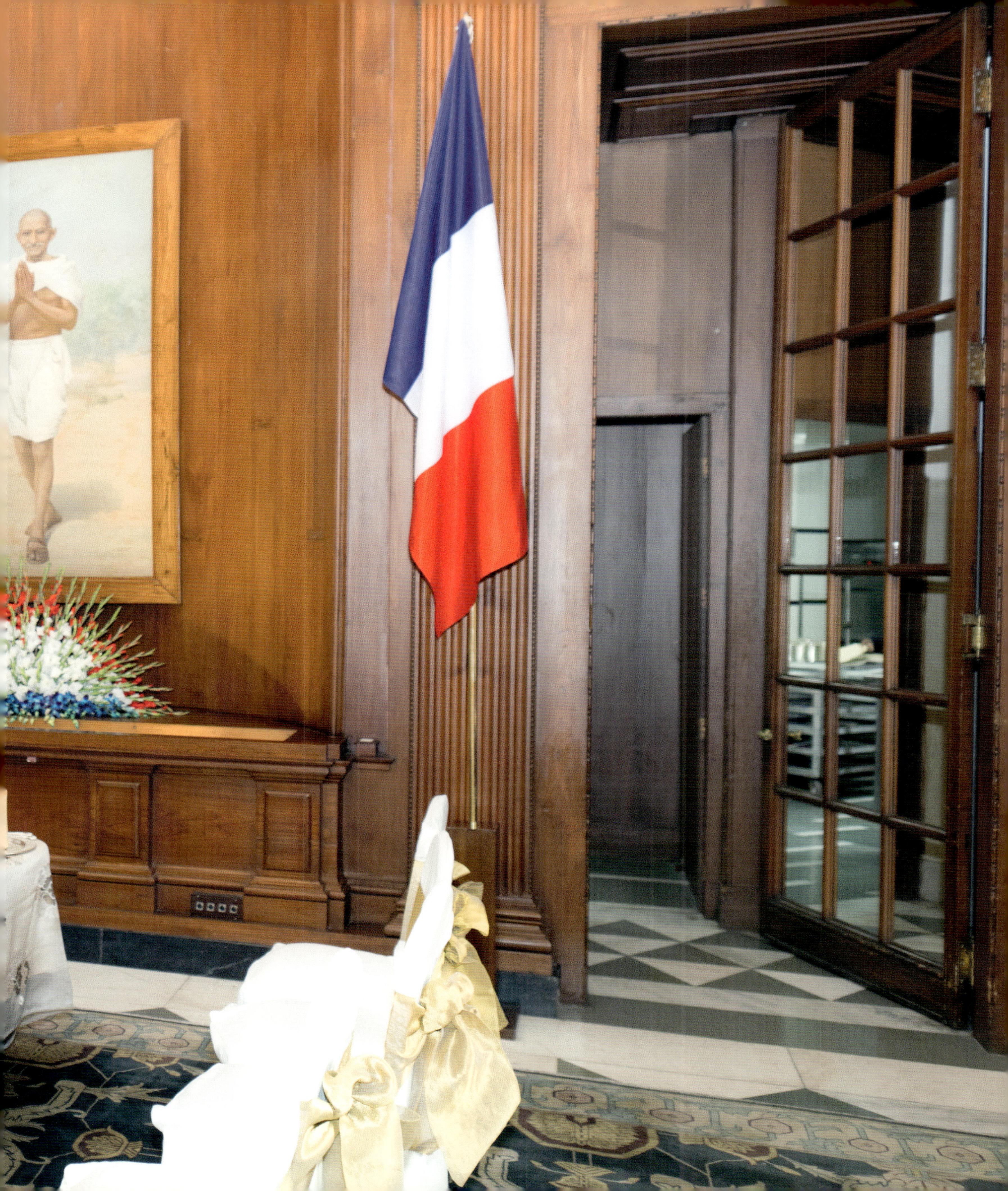

It was also President Patil who hung a portrait of Gandhi where the gold plate donated by the Company of Goldsmiths and Silversmiths was displayed in viceregal times.[45] President Kalam broke out of the stiffness of the banquet hall altogether and held state dinners for Presidents George Bush and Jacques Chirac outside at small, more intimate tables.[46] He also organised the opening of the Kitchen Museum which displays kitchen items and dinnerware from viceregal times. President Pranab Mukherjee has built a new ceremonial hall which can accommodate more guests. This is where he entertained President Barack Obama in January 2015.

The Rashtrapati Bhavan and the Celebration of the Republic

Over the six decades since Independence the Indian Republic has developed its own ceremonial language. Every year garden parties for thousands of guests are held in the Mughal Garden on 26 January and 15 August to celebrate the two most important political moments in the life of the Republic: the ratification of the Indian Constitution and Indian Independence.

Republic and Independence Days are the busiest times of year for the Rashtrapati Bhavan kitchens. Haider recalled that he and his fellow cooks used to begin making samosas for the garden parties two days in advance. Preparing for the August garden party was such hot and stressful work that the cooks were given an air-conditioned room to work in to spare them from cooking such vast quantities of food in the stuffy heat of the basement kitchens. Nowadays the chef and his team of cooks work through the night to prepare for the garden parties. On the day itself, food stands line the paths and guests receive piping hot samosas, freshly cooked on the spot. Haider used to make tamarind chutney to accompany the samosas. Prepared according to his own special recipe using 14 different spices, raisins and jaggery, this was popular among the guests.[47] The garden parties are held in the late afternoon and the eager guests throng the food stalls. There is agreement among the regular guests at the garden parties that the food has become more adventurous. Alongside the standard fare of samosas and gulab jamuns, the guests are presented with more modern and sophisticated bhutta roti rolls, miniature tarts and koftas and Bengali latikas.

The Mughal Garden decorated for a garden party

LEFT & ABOVE: Gardeners carry strands of marigold and wheel barrows of flowers into the garden in preparation for a Republic Day garden party

Gardeners prepare marigolds for the garden decorations

ABOVE: Guests help themselves to food at a garden party LEFT & FACING PAGE: Butlers offer snacks to guests at a garden party

ABOVE: Guests help themselves to food in the banquet hall after a ceremony for freedom fighters

ABOVE: The President's Bodyguard watch over the guests at a garden party; LEFT: Guests crowd into the banquet hall on a wet Independence Day

Notes

1. Eve Curie, *Journey among Warriors* (William Heineman, London, 1943), 449.
2. Interview in Hindi with Kundan Singh, 7 August 2014.
3. Interview with Minhaj Ali.
4. Gyanwati Darbar, ed., *Portrait of a President. Letters of Dr Rajendra Prasad written to Mrs Gyanwati Darbar*, 2 Vols. (Vikas, Delhi, 1974), I, ix.
5. Curie, *Journey among Warriors*, 449.
6. Interview in Hindi with Karimullah, 7 August 2014.
7. Darbar, *Portrait of a President*, I, 34.
8. Venkataraman, *My Presidential Years*, 51.
9. C. Rajagopalchari Papers, Sas. File 76, Records Room, Rashtrapati Bhavan, 42.
10. Interview in English with writers and artists in residence, 21 March 2015.
11. Rakesh Krishnan Simha, 'The Russians are coming!', *Russia and India Report*, 11 July 2014, rbth.com/blogs/2014/07/11/the_russians_are_coming_36615
12. Interview with Abdul Majeed.
13. Ramesh Chandra and Neela Gokhale, eds., *First Woman President of India, Pratibha Patil* (Kalpaz Publications, Delhi, 2008), 159.
14. Sarila, *Once a Prince*, 249.
15. Albala, 'The historical models of food and power', 24.
16. Conversation in English with Anshul Avijit, 11 March 2015.
17. Darbar, *Portrait of a President*, I, 44–45.
18. Ibid., 45.
19. Interview in English with Gaitri Issar Kumar, 27 March 2015.
20. Chandra and Gokhale, *First Woman President*, 159.
21. Interview in Hindi with Biswajeet Barua, 7 August 2014.
22. http://timesofindia.com/home/sunday-times/deep-focus/Prime-perk-A-house-for-the-First-Citizen/articleshow/2062289.cms
23. Banquet menus for Adolfo López Mateos, 6 October 1962, and for Dr Fazil Kutchuk of Cyprus, March 1963, Records Room, Rashtrapati Bhavan.
24. Anjoli Ela Menon, 'The age that was', http://www.india-seminar.com/2002/515/515%20anjolie%20ela%20menon.htm
25. Ruchi Srivastava, 'Carry on Jeeves', *Times of India*, 29 April 2005, http://timesofindia.indiatimes.com/delhi-times/Carry-on-Jeeves/articleshow/1093563.cms
26. Menu of banquet for the president of Yugoslavia, 10 March 1966, and menus for the visit of the king of Bhutan, 17 April 1966, Records Room, Rashtrapati Bhavan.
27. Interview in Hindi with Haider Ali, 29 November 2014.
28. Interview in Hindi with Dooj Prakash, 9 December 2014.
29. Penderel Moon, ed., *Wavell. The Viceroy's Journal* (OUP, Oxford, 1997), 40.
30. Sarila, *Once a Prince*, 240.
31. Interview with Dooj Prakash.
32. Venkantaraman, *My Presidential Years*, 62, 107.
33. Interview in Hindi with Basheer Ahmed, 17 August 2014.
34. Interview in English with Anita Bimal, 4 December 2014.
35. Dasgupta, Debarshi, 'Masala dosa at midnight', *Outlook*, 2 July 2007, http://www.outlookindia.com/article/Masala-Dosa-At-Midnight/234983.
36. Interview with Haider Ali; interview with Razi Haider.
37. Interview with Minhaj Ali.
38. Interview with Razi Haider.
39. Arthur Barlow to his parents, 29 December 1930, Barlow (Hanb) Papers, Centre for South Asian Studies, Cambridge, Box 1, Letter I, 67.
40. Notebook compiled by Major Meysey George Dallas Clive (1907–43): compiled while ADC to Viceroy Lord Willingdon detailing alterations to the Viceroy's House by Lady Willingdon, Mss. Eur. F660, BL.
41. Anjoli Ela Menon, 'The age that was'.
42. Dairy Animals of the President of the Republic of India, from the Office of the President's Bodyguard to the Secretary to the President, 14 May 1968, and Military Secretary to the President to the Commandant of RVC Centre and School, Meerut cantonment, September 1967, Records Room, Rashtrapati Bhavan.
43. Interview in Hindi with Rajiv Kala, 11 March 2015.
44. Interview in Hindi with Pratibha Patil, 7 October 2014.
45. Ibid.
46. Debarshi, 'Masala dosa at midnight'.
47. Interview with Haider Ali.

The Mughal Garden abandoned as the outdoor venue for an at-home due to inclement weather

Various cooks at work preparing an array of dishes

The main kitchen

CHAPTER 5

A National Cuisine

The rise of Mughlai-Punjabi cuisine at the Rashtrapati Bhavan

Traditionally royal courts act as the site where national cuisines are formed.[1] A variety of sophisticated cuisines developed at India's various regional courts. However, as the subcontinent was not ruled by one central power, no all-India national cuisine emerged. Under the British, the cuisine of the Indian government was European. This meant that in the 1960s, when the Indian government began to assert Indian food as the representative cuisine, no core repertoire of dishes common to all of India existed to which they could refer. In search of grand Indian dishes suitable for state banquets the cooks at the palace turned to Mughal cuisine for inspiration. One of the first state banquets to feature Indian food on the menu sandwiched a biryani in between French onion soup and a British-style cream tuti fruiti dessert. Biryani is one of Mughal cuisine's signature dishes, the product of the meeting of Persian pilau with spicy north Indian rice dishes in Emperor Akbar's kitchens. The biryani was accompanied by aloo dum, cooked under pressure according to a technique perfected in the 18th century at the Mughal satellite court of Awadh. North Indian naan breads were also served.

This feast was almost certainly prepared under the guidance of Shafiullah, an expert in Mughlai cuisine who was recruited by President Prasad. On a visit to the nizam of Hyderabad, President Prasad was so impressed by the sophistication and deliciousness of the food at the nizam's court that he met with his cook and asked him to come and work for him in Delhi. Shafiullah is said to have been rather reluctant to leave his home but he eventually arrived at the Rashtrapati Bhavan just as President Prasad's term of office was drawing to a close. He stayed on and worked for President Radhakrishnan. He introduced to the Rashtrapati Bhavan kitchens the fragrant Hyderabadi dish of succulent mutton layered with aromatic rice, kachche gosht ki biryani, and its natural accompaniment, mirchi ka salan. This was a salan that was traditionally made only for royalty with a yoghurt rather than a coconut base. Shafiullah was also a master of Awadhi qormas rich in the cream that the dairy-loving Awadhis relished, thickened, Persian-style, with almonds. During Fakhruddin Ali Ahmed's presidency a cook was recruited from Lucknow who excelled in making shaami kebabs, crispy on the outside but so soft and silky within that even the toothless 18th-century king Asaf-ud-Daulah used to eat them with pleasure.[2] The soft melt-in-the mouth galouti kababs made with lamb and raw papayas that are the product of the kitchens today continue this Awadhi tradition.

Some people credit Shafiullah with introducing the Punjabi tandoor to the kitchens of the Rashtrapati Bhavan. The first menu in the Rashtrapati Bhavan archives which mentions tandoori food is the March 1963 banquet for the vicepresident of Cyprus.[3] This would suggest that the tandoor was introduced to the Rashtrapati Bhavan in the early presidential years. Desai Ram, who began his career as a cook's mate in 1958, recalled that it was equipped with one large underground tandoor and two small tandoors.[4] Lalit Joshi, general manager of the India International Centre, and in earlier years a frequent guest at Rashtrapati Bhavan banquets, recalled that in those days tandoori food was a novelty.[5] But if it was a novelty to Indian guests, tandoori food was familiar to many of the foreign dignitaries due to the popularity of the tandoor oven in Indian restaurants around the world. Indeed, for many of the visiting dignitaries at this time Indian food was synonymous with tandoori chicken and naan breads.[6]

Tandoori specialities are still comfortingly familiar to many of the Rashtrapati Bhavan's foreign guests. The main kitchens in the basement are equipped with two tandoor ovens and there are two in the butler's pantry next to the banquet hall. This means that the breads for the banquet arrive at the table still hot from the oven. Highlights of the meal for the emir of Qatar in March 2015 were the fish tikka and the vegetarian equivalent of paneer, peppers and pineapple which had been steeped in an exquisite marinade before being cooked in the tandoor. The tandoori marinade is also used on mushrooms which are then stuffed and baked in the oven to produce one of the Rashtrapati Bhavan's signature vegetarian dishes.

The popularity of tandoor cookery and the fact that the dishes complement and combine well with those of Mughlai cuisine meant that by the 1970s the high-status cuisine of India was a combination of Mughlai and Punjabi. This was the cuisine which in urban areas came to be seen as most appropriate on formal occasions and which dominated the menus of many restaurants, even in regions with their own strong and distinctive culinary traditions. Even in notoriously foodie Bengal, the regional dishes people would have enjoyed in their homes were only considered suitable for low-brow eating places.[7] The result was that for the first four decades after Independence, Delhi-Punjabi prevailed as the high-status cuisine. A combination which dominated not just cookery but many other areas of Indian culture.

Sumptuous Mughlai-Punjabi specialities graced the banquet menus of the Rashtrapati Bhavan throughout the 1970s and 80s. Visiting dignitaries were treated to Punjabi-style burra kebabs and Mughlai navratan qormas and chicken shahjahani.[8] Minhaj recalled the anarkali chicken the cooks used to prepare, stuffed with almonds and raisins, rolled up and cooked in a nut gravy. 'Our Mughlai used to be the best,' he recalled.[9] Haider Ali who joined the kitchens in the late 1960s when Zakir Husain was president, was a master of the courtly Mughlai-Punjabi cuisine. He even invented a new Mughlai-style dish called zill-e-darvesh made with almonds, milk and sugar. It had a lacy texture caused by pouring hot desi ghee over the mixture.[10] (See recipe in chapter 4)

The quality of food at the Rashtrapati Bhavan reflected not only the skill of the cooks but also the amount of interest the presidential wives took in the kitchens. The wives and daughters of the early presidents did not play an active part in political life and their sphere of influence was limited to the president's private kitchen. This situation changed with the presidency of Fakhruddin Ali Ahmed. His wife took a lively interest in the kitchens. Haider recalled that the kitchen staff were surprised when Begum Abida Ahmed called a meeting with the cooks to discuss the banquet to be given for the shah of Iran in October 1974. None of the other first ladies had shown any interest in the kitchens. Together, Begum Ahmed and the cooks planned a menu to celebrate the ancient links between India and Iran. Before the banquet they cooked sample dishes and held a special tasting session to choose which ones they would serve. Haider prepared the Hyderabadi speciality of chicken nihari, and an Awadhi slow-cooked dum pukht. To accompany them he made sweet, flaky, saffron-flavoured sheermal breads. From then on Begum Ahmed played an important role in the kitchens, encouraging the cooks to excel, helping to choose banquet menus and organising tasting sessions.[11]

Shorshe Bata Maach (Mustard Fish Curry)

This signature Bengali fish curry has been added to the Rashtrapati Bhavan repertoire in honour of President Pranab Mukherjee.

Ingredients

4 medium-size fillets of rohu without bones * 1 tsp turmeric powder* 4 tsp mustard seeds * 2 tbsp poppy seeds * 4–5 split green chillies * 2 tbsp mustard oil * 1 tsp turmeric powder * salt to taste *

Method

Clean fillets of fish and rub with a little salt and turmeric powder and set aside for 10 minutes.
Make a paste of the mustard seeds, add a little salt and leave for 15 minutes.
Make a paste of the poppy seeds with a little water and salt.
Heat 2 tbsp mustard oil in a pan.
Fry the fish carefully on medium heat till the fish turns golden brown.
Remove the fish from the oil and keep aside.
Now add the poppy seed paste and cook for a minute.
Add salt, turmeric powder and the green chillies.
Add the mustard paste to the gravy along with 3 cups of water and bring to the boil.
Add the fish pieces and coat them in the gravy.
Serve with plain boiled rice.

LEFT: Freedom fighters enjoying Rashtrapati Bhawan snacks at an at-home to celebrate the 73rd anniversary of the Quit India movement

Showcasing India at the Rashtrapati Bhavan

The officials and cooks who plan the menus for state banquets are acutely conscious that they are putting Indian culture on show. The vast and varied nature of India has to be conveyed to visiting dignitaries in a few short days, normally spent mainly in New Delhi. The state banquet is an opportunity to give the visitor a sense of the vibrancy of India's various cuisines. At a luncheon for the Soviet prime minister, Nikolai Ryzhkov, President Venkataraman was pleased to find that 'Mrs Ryzhkov, who sat on my right, expressed more interest in the different types of dishes served than in national and international issues.'[22] She particularly liked the idlis and admired the roses from the Mughal Garden. Shashi Tharoor describes India not as a melting pot but as 'a thali a selection of sumptuous dishes in different bowls. Each tastes different and does not necessarily mix with the next, but they belong together on the same plate, and they complement each other in making the meal a satisfying repast.'[23] Increasingly the banqueting table has become a symbolic national thali as the once dominant Mughlai-Punjabi cuisine has given way to menus which mix and match foods from a variety of regions to create a harmonious medley. The banquet for General Musharraf in 2001 was a spectacular mix with Nepalese chicken dumplings, south Indian dosas, Goan prawns, Tamil chicken chettinad, Kashmiri kebabs, Amritsari fish, Gujarati pigeon pea dal dokhli, and ending with the regal Mughlai shahi tukra.[24]

ABOVE: Food diplomacy in action. President Mukherjee in conversation with Mohammed bin Zayed al Nahyan at a luncheon held in his honour on 11 February 2016; LEFT: Guests arrive for a state banquet

Guests take their seat at the banquet table

Indian society does not have a long tradition of forging sociable bonds through commensality. In the past, caste and community customs and practices positively discouraged the sharing among strangers of food around a table. British officials were often offended when their Indian hosts refused to partake of a meal in their presence. But by the time India achieved Independence, India's new rulers understood the importance of international dining culture and became comfortable with different dinner companions. State banquets are a stylised enactment of status and respect. A glamorous dinner for a visiting dignitary signals membership of both the host and the guest in an exclusive group. India's new rulers understood that commensality was vital to international diplomacy.

Great care is taken at state banquets to complement and acknowledge the guest and his country. In March 2015 the Sri Lankan president was delighted by the bhagara baigan served at the banquet in his honour because aubergine is his favourite vegetable. At a banquet for the king of Bhutan, he was touched that the table decorations echoed the yellow and orange of Bhutan's flag.[25] The work that goes into making a banquet a success is largely backstage. The catering department of the comptroller, the additional comptroller, the naval catering supervisors, the cooks, the bakers and halwais, the butlers, the sound and light technicians, the staff who clean and maintain the rooms and the equipment, all are inconspicuous and largely unacknowledged masters of food diplomacy. Like the Saraswati River, flowing invisibly below India's surface, food diplomacy flows below the more obvious work of political diplomacy.[26] Although the new Republic of India inherited much of its banqueting tradition from the British, from the soup at the beginning of the meal, the elaborately folded napkins, the butler service and the division of the meal into courses, to the toast in honour of the visiting dignitary, the Rashtrapati Bhavan has evolved its own unique banqueting style. A banquet at the president's palace is now a decidedly Indian affair which presents its guest of honour with a window onto Indian culture.

Notes

1. Norbert Elias, *The Civilizing Process. The History of Manners and State Formation and Civilization*, 1st published 1939 (Blackwell, Oxford, 1994), 266–67.
2. Interview with Haider Ali.
3. Banquet menu for Fazil Kutchuk of Cyprus.
4. Interview in Hindi with Desai Ram, 17 August 2014.
5. Conversation in English with Lalit Joshi, 10 March 2015.
6. Ashis Nandy, 'The changing popular culture of Indian food: preliminary notes', *South Asia Research* 24 1 (2004), 9–19, 14.
7. Ibid.
8. Banquet menus for the king and queen of Nepal, 6 March 1980, for the prime minister of Mauritius, 28 October 1980, and for the president of Palestine, 26 March 1990, Records Room, Rashtrapati Bhavan.
9. Interview with Minhaj Ali.
10. Interview with Haider Ali.
11. Ibid.
12. Arjun Appadurai, 'How to make a national cuisine: cookbooks in contemporary India', *Comparative Studies in Society and History* 30, s1 (1988), 3–24.
13. Banquet menus for Yasser Arafat, 26 March 1990, and for Nelson Mandela, 15 October 1990, Records Room, Rashtrapati Bhavan.
14. Venkataraman, *My Presidential Years*, 104.
15 Banquet menus for Yasser Arafat, and for Nelson Mandela.
16. Venkantamaran, *My Presidential Years*, 165.
17. Kishore Singh, 'Flavours of the Rashtrapati Bhavan', *Business Standard*, 28 July 2012, http://www.business-standard.com/article/opinion/kishore-singh-flavours-of-rashtrapati-bhavan-112072800037_1.html
18. Banquet menus for Queen Elizabeth II, 13 October 1997, and for General Musharraf, 14 July 2001, Records Room, Rashtrapati Bhavan.
19. Crimson Chakra, Chef Jacob, http://www.crimsonchakra.in/page/crimson-chakra---chef-jacob; Shonali Muthalaly, 'All Spiced Up', *The Hindu*, 21 May 2014.
20. Interview with President Patil.
21. Chitra Banerji, *Land of Milk and Honey. Travels in the history of Indian food* (Seagull Books, London, 2007), 1–26; speech by Meira Kumar at Rashtrapati Bhavan, 19 March 2015.
22. Venkataraman, *My Presidential Years*, 104.
23. Shashi Tharoor, *The Elephant, the Tiger and the Cellphone. Reflections on India, the Emerging 21st Century Power* (Skyhorse Publishing, New York, 2011), 62.
24. Banquet menu for General Musharraf,
25. Interview in English with Lieutenant Commander Rakesh Yadav.
26. Interview in English with Karan Singh, 26 March 2015.

Bibliography

I. PUBLISHED SOURCES

Albala, Ken. 'The historical models of food and power in European courts of the nineteenth century: an expository essay and prologue'. Daniëlle de Vooght, ed. *Royal Taste. Food, Power and Status at the European Courts after 1789.* Ashgate, Farnham, Surrey, 2011.

Appadurai, Arjun. 'How to make a national cuisine: cookbooks in contemporary India'. *Comparative Studies in Society and History* 30, 1 (1998).

Banerji, Chitrita, *Land of Milk and Honey. Travels in the History of Indian Food*. London: Seagull Books, 2007.

Beaton, Cecil. *Indian Diary and Album*. Oxford: OUP, 1991.

Bence-Jones, Mark. *Palaces of the Raj. Magnificence and Misery of the Lord Sahibs*. London: George Allen and Unwin, 1973.

Byron, Robert. 'New Delhi II—The interior of the viceroy's house'. *Country Life*, LXIX, No. 1795, 13 June 1931.

Cannadine, David. *Ornamentalism. How the British Saw Their Empire*. London: Allen Lane, 2001.

Chandra, Ramesh and Neela Gokhale, eds. *First Woman President of India, Pratibha Patil*. Delhi: Kalpaz Publications, 2008.

Close, H.M. *Attlee, Wavell and the Transfer of Power*. Islamabad: National Book Foundation, 1997.

Coats, Peter. *Of Generals and Gardens. The Autobiography of Peter Coats*. London: Weidenfeld and Nicolson, 1976.

Curie, Eve. *Journey Among Warriors*. London: William Heineman, 1943.

Darbar, Gyanwati, ed. *Portrait of a President. Letters of Dr Rajendra Prasad written to Mrs Gyanwati Darbar*, 2 vols. Delhi: Vikas, 1974.

Davis, Wendy M. *Dal and Rice*. Motreal: McGill-Queen's University Press, 2009.

Elias, Norbert. *The Civilizing Process. The History of Manners and State Formation and Civilization*. 1st published 1939. Oxford: Blackwell, 1994.

Fort, Adrian. *Wavell. The Life and Times of an Imperial Servant*. London: Jonathan Cape, 2009.

Hunt, Tristram. *Ten Cities that Made an Empire*. Londo: Penguin, 2015.

Jones, Kathryn. *For the Royal Table. Dining at the Palace*. London: Royal Collection Publications, 2008.

Kumar, Meira. *Indian Parliamentary Diplomacy. Speaker's Perspective*. New Delhi: Lok Sabha Secretariat, 2015.

Ludington, Charles C. 'Drinking for approval: wine and the British court from George III to Victoria and Albert'. Daniëlle de Vooght, ed. *Royal Taste. Food, Power and Status at the European Courts after* 1789. Ashgate, Farnham, Surrey, 2011.

Moon, Penderel, ed. *Wavell. The Viceroy's Journal*. Oxford: OUP, 1997.

Morgan, Linda. 'Diplomatic gastronomy: style and power at the table'. *Food and Foodways* 20, 2 (2012).

Mountbatten, Pamela. *India Remembered*. London: Pavilion, 2007.

Nandy, Ashis. 'The changing popular culture of Indian food: preliminary notes'. *South Asia Research* 24, 1 (2004).

Pellenc, Baron Jean. *Diamonds and Dust. India through French Eyes*. London: John Murray, 1936.

Ram, Indrani Jagjivan. *Milestones. A Memoir*. New Delhi: Penguin, 2010.

Sambrook, Pamela A. and Peter Brears, ed. *The Country House Kitchen 1650–1900*. Stroud: The History Press, 2010.

Sarila Narendra Singh. *Once a Prince of Sarila. Of Palaces and Tiger Hunts, of Nehrus and Mountbattens*. London: I.B. Tauris, 2008.

Satow, Ernest. *Guide to Diplomatic Practice*. 1st published 1917. Cambridge: Cambridge University Press, 2011.

Schwartz, Stuart B, ed., *Tropical Babylons. Sugar and the Making of the Atlantic World, 1450–1680*. Chapel Hill & London: The University of North Carolina Press, 2004.

Sharar, Abdul Halim. *Lucknow. The Last Phase of an Oriental Culture*. Ed., E.S. Harcourt. Trans. Fakhir Hussain. Delhi:

Oxford University Press, 1989.

Stols, Eddy. 'The expansion of the sugar market in Western Europe'. Ed., Stuart B. Schwartz. *Tropical Babylons. Sugar and the Making of the Atlantic World, 1450–1680*. Chapel Hill & London: The University of North Carolina Press, 2004.

Tharoor, Shashi. *The Elephant, the Tiger and the Cellphone. Reflections on India, the Emerging 21st century power*. New York: Skyhorse Publishing, 2011.

Venkataraman, R. *My Presidential* Year. New Delhi: Indus, 1994.

Vooght, Daniëlle de, ed. *Royal Taste. Food, Power and Status at the European Courts after 1789*. Ashgate, Farnham, Surrey, 2011.

Wohlwahsen, Andreas. *Imperial Delhi. The British Capital of the Indian Empire*. London: Prestel, 2002.

Wolpert, Stanley. *Nehru. A Tryst with Destiny*. Oxford: OUP, 1996

II NEWSPAPER ARTICLES AND ONLINE SOURCES

'A house for the first citizen'. http://timesofindia.com/home/sunday-times/deep-focus/Prime-perk-A-house-for-the-First-Citizen/articleshow/2062289.cms

Dasgupta, Debarshi. 'Masala dosa at midnight'. *Outlook*, 2 July 2007. http://www.outlookindia.com/article/Masala-Dosa-At-Midnight/234983

French, Patrick. 'Goat's curd, Mr Viceroy?' *The Week*, 15 February 2015.

Chef Jacob. 'Crimson Chakra'. http://www.crimsonchakra.in/page/crimson-chakra---chef-jacob

Menon, Anjoli Ela. 'The age that was'. http://www.india-seminar.com/2002/515/515%20anjolie%20ela%20menon.htm

Muthalaly, Shonali. 'All Spiced Up'. *The Hindu*, 21 May 2014. Sciolino, Elaine. 'Club des Chefs des Chefs'. *Lumière*, 27 July 2013.

Simha, Rakesh Krishnan. 'The Russians are coming!' *Russia and India Report*, 11 July 2014. rbth.com/blogs/2014/07/11/the_russians_are_coming_36615

Singh, Kishore. 'Flavours of the Rashtrapati Bhavan'. *Business Standard*, 28 July 2012. http://www.business-standard.com/article/opinion/kishore-singh-flavours-of-rashtrapati-bhavan-112072800037_1.html

Srivastava, Ruchi, 'Carry on Jeeves'. *Times of India*, 29 April 2005. http://timesofindia.indiatimes.com/delhi-times/Carry-on-Jeeves/articleshow/1093563.cms

III. PRIMARY SOURCES

Government Papers

Files, Records Room, Rashtrapati Bhavan

India Office Records, British Library

National Archives of India, New Delhi

Private Papers

Oriental and India Office Collections, British Library, London

Halifax Papers, Mss. Eur. C152

Papers of Sir Samuel Hoare, Secretary of State for India 1931–35, 1931–54, Mss. Eur. E240

Notebook compiled by Major Meysey George Dallas Clive (1907–43), Mss. Eur. F660

Patrick Henry James Southby Papers, Mss. Eur. T212

Diary of Sir Francis Cannon Tudsbery (1888–1968), Mss. Eur. F679

Letter Willingdon to Hoare, 24 October 1931, Mss. Eur. E240/5

Centre for South Asian Studies, Cambridge

Barlow (Hanb) Papers

Mrs Viola Bayley, Microfilm Box 7, No. 57

Hall Papers

McKnight Papers

Sir Peter Norton-Griffiths Papers

Private Collections

Bird, Tom, *Letters Home 1939–46* (privately printed, 1996)

Letters by George and Enid Boon

Interviews

Interview in Hindi with Abdul Majeed, 9 June 2014.

Interview in Hindi with Biswajeet Barua, 7 August 2014.

Interview in Hindi with Minhaj Ali, 7 August 2014 and 4 January 2016.

Interview in Hindi with Karimullah, 7 August 2014.

Interview in Hindi with Kundan Singh, 7 August 2014.

Interview in Hindi with Basheer Ahmed, 17 August 2014.

Interview in Hindi with Biren Barua, 17 August 2014.

Interview in Hindi with Desai Ram, 17 August 2014.

Interview in Hindi with Haider Ali, 29 November 2014.

Interview in Hindi with Pratibha Patil, 7 October 2014.

Interview in English with Anita Bimal, 4 December 2014.

Interview in Hindi with Dooj Prakash, 9 December 2014.

Conversation in English with Lalit Joshi, 10 March 2015.

Conversation in English with Anshul Avijit, 11 March 2015.

Interview in English with Lieutenant Commander Rakesh Yadav, 17 March 2015.

Interview in English with Gaitri Issar Kumar, 27 March 2015.

Interview in English with Tom A. Bird, 4 June 2015.

Interview in English with Machindra Kasture, 10 March 2015.

Interview in Hindi with Rajiv Kala, 11 March 2015.

Interview in English with writers and artists in residence, 21 March 2015.

Interview in English with Karan Singh, 26 March 2015.

Interview in Hindi with Razi Haider, 4 January 2016.

Interview in Hindi with Ashish Kumar, 4 January 2016.

Interview in English with Montu Saini, 4 January 2016.

Interview in Hindi and English with Vikash, 4 January 2016.

Interview in English with Captain Prashant Singh, 5 January 2016.

Interview in English with Major Rajesh Kumar, Lieutenant Commander Rakesh Yadav, Major R K Banu Chander and sSquadron Leader Yash Aryan, 18 January 2016.

Acknowledgements

We would like to thank the many people who have helped with the writing of this volume, one of a series commissioned by the President's Secretariat and IGNCA (including the steering committee for the project) and produced by Sahapedia.

This volume was made possible by the cooperation of the resource people at the Rashtrapati Bhavan, Gaitri Isaar Kumar (Joint Secretary-cum-Social Secretary to the President), Captain Prashant Singh (Comptroller of the President's Household) and Anita Bimal (Additional Comptroller of the President's Household), who were extremely generous with their time and assistance. We are also indebted to the staff of the Records Room and Photo Section. We would like to thank the ADCs to the president, Squadron Leader Abhinav Bhattacharya, Lieutenant Commander Rakesh Yadav, Major Shobhit Pandey, Major Rajesh Kumar, Major R.K. Banu Chander and Squadron Leader Yash Aryan. Our wholehearted thank to Chefs Machindra Kasture and Montu Saini, all the cooks, bakers, butlers and household staff, past and present, who cheerfully gave us their help while plying us with delicious food.

At Sahapedia, we would like to thank the project director, Sudha Gopalakrishnan, and the project team, including Shambwaditya Ghosh, Devorica Adhikari, Gaurav Ujjainwal, Sunny Jain, Aruna Ghose, Malini Saigal and Shruti Tomar. In particular, we would like to thank Yashaswini Chandra for her superb efficiency while coordinating the work on the volume, which she did with patience and grace.

We are grateful to our invaluable researchers Ram Niwas Singh, Habiba Insaf and Suchismita Chatopadhyay. Special thanks are due to Suchismita for making Lizzie's research trip to Delhi both fruitful and enjoyable. It was a pleasure to work with our photographer, Dheeraj Paul, who remained good humoured throughout while producing fine photographs.

We would like to thank the staff and librarians of the following libraries and archives: in Britain, Cambridge University Library, the British Library, the Imperial War Museum Photography Section, Southampton University Library, and the Centre for South Asian Studies, Cambridge University. In Delhi, Sahitya Akademi, Kala Nidhi Library (IGNCA), Hamdard Central Library, the Gymkhana Club Library, the National Archives of India, the Nehru Memorial Library and Museum. We would also like to thank e-books from DELNET.

We are grateful to everyone who generously gave their time to be interviewed, they are named throughout the text. For their assistance we would also like to thank Anshul Avijit, Naman Ahuja, the late Chris Bayly, Peter Boon, Sarah Burwood, William Dalrymple, Sir Gerald Eliot, Narayani Gupta, Kevin Greenbank, John Hay, Rosie Llewellyn-Jones, Partha Mitter, Pushpesh Pant, John C. Richardson, Thomas Seidel, Shukla at Lutyens' Bungalow, Sarah Squires, Major Narindar Saroop, Barry Williamson and Gillian Wright.

Index